# Happily
# *Even* After

## The Guide to Divorce in New Jersey

D1157487

# CARL TAYLOR III, ESQ.

**CARL TAYLOR LAW**
908-237-3096
www.mynjdivorcelawyer.com

Country Side Plaza North
361 State Route 31
Building E, Suite 1501
Flemington, NJ 08822

ISBN: 978-1-63385-308-9

*Designed and published by*

Word Association Publishers
205 Fifth Avenue
Tarentum, Pennsylvania 15084

www.wordassociation.com
1.800.827.7903

# Contents

Foreword ........................................................................ xiii

Legal Disclaimer ........................................................... xv

Introduction................................................................... xvi

About Carl A. Taylor III, Esq. .......................................1
    Carl's Credentials ...................................................... 4

About You......................................................................6

Firm Mission Statement: Sharks and Dolphins .........10

New Jersey Divorce and Family Law.........................13
    Efficient Solutions ..................................................... 15

Seven Simple Steps to Take before Filing a Divorce... And Ten
Things That Might Surprise You about Divorce in New Jersey .16
    Seven Simple Steps to Take before Filing a Divorce ............ 16
        1. Keep a Journal/Log........................................ 17
        2. Don't Lose Your Temper ................................ 18
        3. Consider Meeting with a Mental Health Expert.......... 18
        4. Be Very Careful When Using Social Media.................. 18
        5. Take Notes and Store Documents in a Safe Location . 19
        6. Get Your Finances in Order ............................ 19
        7. Don't Be Afraid to Ask Your Attorney Questions.......... 20
    Ten Things That May Surprise You about a
    New Jersey Divorce ................................................. 21
        1. Fault Isn't That Important.............................. 21
        2. The Laws Are (Essentially) Gender Neutral ............... 21

3. There's Probably Not a Conspiracy ............................. 22

4. The Judge Likely Won't Speak
with Your Children ................................................. 22

5. You Can Sue or Be Sued for a Marital Tort ................. 22

6. Children May Not Be Emancipated at
Age Eighteen or Even Twenty-one ............................. 23

7. Lawyers Cannot Represent Both Parties ..................... 23

8. Grandparents Will Often Have no Rights
of Visitation without a Court Order—And That
Will Be Difficult to Obtain .................................... 23

9. Divorces Can Take More than a Year ........................ 24

10. Prenuptial Agreements Are Becoming
More Common .................................................. 24

**The Heart of the Matter—Addressing the
Emotional Side of a Divorce** .................................... **25**
*Balancing Emotion with Proper Boundaries Can Lead
to the Optimum Outcome* ..................................... 25

**Divorce FAQs** ..................................................... **28**
Q. How long will it take to be divorced? ......................... 28

Q. What are the legal fees involved in
getting divorced? ............................................. 29

Q. What are my responsibilities while
the divorce is pending? ........................................ 29

Q. What if someone commits an
act of domestic violence? ..................................... 29

Q. Will I be entitled to custody and parenting time? ...... 30

Q. How is child support calculated? ........................... 30

Q. How will I know if I'm entitled to alimony
or if I have to pay alimony? ................................... 30

Q. Why should I choose Carl Taylor Law, LLC
for my divorce? ............................................... 31

Q. What should I bring to an initial consultation
about a divorce? ........................................................... 31

Q. What will you ask me during the initial
divorce consultation? ................................................... 32

A Note on New Jersey Divorce: Initial Consultation ............. 33
FAQ Conclusion ....................................................... 33

**What if I'm Not Ready to Get Divorced Yet?** ...........................**34**
Saving the Marriage ... or Not ................................................ 35
Should I Discuss My Desire to Divorce with My Spouse? ..... 36
To What Extent Should Emotion Fuel a Divorce? ................. 38
But Don't Be a Pushover ......................................................... 40
A Word on Reconciliation ........................................................ 42
Endings Are Important in New Jersey Divorce Law ............. 43

**What Factors May Complicate a New Jersey Divorce?** .............**46**
What Can Be Done to Simplify a New Jersey Divorce? ........ 47
Conclusion ............................................................................... 48

**Does My Spouse Have to Retain an Attorney?** .........................**49**
**Conclusion** ................................................................. **50**

**Helping Children through a Divorce**
**An Interview with Glenn Murphy, MA, LPC** ...........................**51**
Interview Transcript ................................................................ 52
Mediation–Coaching and Counseling ................................... 59
Splitting the Family ................................................................. 61
Stormy Relationships .............................................................. 62

**The Nuts and Bolts of the New Jersey Divorce Procedure** ........**64**
Basic Outline of a New Jersey Divorce ................................. 64
Grounds for Divorce in New Jersey ....................................... 66
    1. Irreconcilable Differences ............................................. 66
    2. No Fault ........................................................................ 67
    3. Extreme Mental or Physical Cruelty .............................. 67
    4. Adultery ........................................................................ 67
    5. Other Grounds .............................................................. 68

*Uncontested Divorces* ............................................................. 68

*New Jersey Uncontested-Divorce Hearings* ........................ 69

*Mediation* ............................................................................. 70

*After the Uncontested-Divorce Hearing* ............................... 70

**The 11-Step Divorce Litigation Process .................................. 72**

*Step 1: Is Divorce Really the Answer?* ................................... 72

*Step 2: Choosing an Attorney* ................................................ 73

*Step 3: Pleadings and the Case Information Statement* ....... 74

    *Res Judicata and the Entire Controversy Doctrine* ......... 75

    *Three Major Types of Pleadings in a*

    *New Jersey Divorce* ......................................................... 75

    *Case Information Statement (CIS)* .................................... 76

*Step 4: Case Management Conferences (CMCs)* ................. 77

*Step 5: Beginning Negotiations* ............................................. 77

*Step 6: Discovery* .................................................................... 78

*Step 7: Continuing Negotiations and*

*the Marital Settlement Agreement* .......................................... 79

*Step 8: Early Settlement Panel* ............................................... 81

*Step 9: Court-Ordered Economic Mediation* ........................ 82

*Step 10: Intensive Settlement Conference* ............................ 82

*Step 11: The Trial* .................................................................... 83

*Conclusion* ............................................................................... 83

**An Overview of Relevant New Jersey Divorce Law .................. 84**

*Child Support Law in New Jersey* ........................................... 84

*Determining Child Support in New Jersey* ............................. 84

*Deviation from the Child-Support Guidelines* ....................... 85

*Modification of Child Support in New Jersey* ........................ 86

*Custody Law in New Jersey* .................................................... 87

*New Jersey Child Custody: Best Interests of the Children*

*Standard* ................................................................................... 88

*Types of Custody* .................................................................... 88

*Gender and Custody* ............................................................... 89

*Modification of New Jersey Child-Custody Decisions* .......... 89

Litigation of Child-Custody Issues in New Jersey ................ 90

    *Newburgh v. Arrigo Factors* ................................. 90

Contributing to a Child's Gap Year ........................... 92

Emancipation and Child Costs ................................ 92

Parental Strain and College Costs .......................... 92

Parenting-Time Law in New Jersey .......................... 93

Basic Concepts of New Jersey Parenting Time ............... 93

Parenting-Time Agreements ................................. 94

Modifying Parenting-Time Agreements ...................... 95

Who Decides the Child's Religious Upbringing? .............. 95

The Role of Courts in Determining New Jersey Divorce

Religious Choice Issues .................................... 96

Who Provides Health Insurance and

Unreimbursed Medical Expenses for the Children? ........... 98

What about after a Divorce Is Finalized? .................. 98

Health Insurance Coverage for a Spouse .................... 98

Health Insurance Coverage for Children .................... 99

Unreimbursed Medical Expenses for Children ............... 99

Conclusion ................................................ 100

**New Jersey Alimony** .......................................... **101**

    **Alimony Defined** ......................................... **101**

    **History of Alimony** ....................................... **102**

    **Alimony Examples** ........................................ **102**

        *The Classic Example* ...................................... 102

        *A More Modern Example* ................................. 103

    Differences between Alimony and Child Support ............. 104

    Duration of Alimony ...................................... 105

    Duration of Alimony—Jim and Jill Analysis ................. 106

    Open-Durational Alimony .................................. 107

    Alimony and Good-Faith Retirement ....................... 107

    Can I Waive Alimony? ..................................... 109

    New Jersey Alimony Reform Act ........................... 110

        *Alimony Is Legally Speaking Now Gender Neutral* ....... 112

        *The Length of the Marriage Is Extremely Important* ..... 112

Good-Faith Retirement, Cohabitation,
and Remarriage ............................................................... 113
Protecting Alimony ................................................................ 114
How the Tax Cut and Jobs Act of 2018 Affected Alimony .. 114
State and Local Tax Deductions and Property Taxes ..... 115
Prenups and Alimony............................................................. 116
Alimony Standard .................................................................. 116
What Are My Responsibilities while the
Divorce is Pending?.............................................................. 117
Alimony at Trial...................................................................... 118
A Quick Note on Exempt Property ....................................... 119
Superseding Alimony Termination Events ........................... 120
Types of Alimony.................................................................... 120
Limited-Durational Alimony ........................................... 121
Open-Durational Alimony ............................................... 121
Rehabilitative Alimony..................................................... 121
Can Fault Impact an Alimony Award? .................................. 122
Modifying Alimony ................................................................ 123
Limited-Durational Alimony Modification ..................... 123
Permanent and Substantial Change
in Circumstances.................................................................... 124
Payment of Alimony............................................................... 125
Alimony Collection Issues ..................................................... 125
How Does Bankruptcy Affect a Divorce
or Support Obligations?........................................................ 126

**Divorce Tips......................................................................... 127**
What Issues Should a Divorce Agreement Address?.......... 127
Standard Divorce Agreement Considerations..................... 127
Child Custody and Parenting Time................................. 127
Alimony ............................................................................ 128
Child Support................................................................... 128
Division of Assets............................................................. 128
Counsel Fees.................................................................... 129

*Future Education Costs*..................................... 129

*Life Insurance Requirements*............................ 129

*Health Insurance/Future Health Costs*............ 129

*Tax Treatment* ................................................. 129

*Education/Child's Surname/Religious Upbringing*....... 130

*Using Civil Litigation Tactics in a High-Conflict Divorce*..... 130

*During the Divorce, Should I Leave the Marital Home?*...... 135

*In Favor of Not Leaving the Marital Residence* ............ 135

*In Favor of Leaving the Marital Residence* .................. 136

*Divorce in the Age of Bitcoin–Divorcing
in the Technological Age*..................................... 137

**Paying for Your Divorce**.............................................. **140**

*Who Pays Counsel Fees in a Divorce?*................... 142

*Which Party Is Responsible for Divorce Counsel Fees?*...... 143

*Collecting Money Due in Family Law Court*........................ 144

*Constructive Trusts*................................................. 145

*Laches*.................................................................. 145

*If One of Us Remarries, Does That Affect Child Support?* ..146

**Types of Experts Available for a Contested
New Jersey Divorce** ...................................................... **150**

*Real Estate Appraisers*........................................... 150

*Forensic Accountants* ............................................ 151

*Child-Custody Experts*............................................ 151

*Appraisers* ............................................................ 151

*Business Appraisers*................................................ 151

*Employment/Employability Experts*........................... 152

**Assets Not Subject to Equitable Distribution**......................... **153**

*Premarital Property* ................................................ 153

*Gifts and Inheritances*............................................. 154

*Personal-Injury Settlements* .................................... 154

*Life Insurance Obligations* ...................................... 155

*Life Insurance during the Divorce Process*................... 155

*Life Insurance during Divorce Negotiations* ........................ 156
*Alimony Deduction Eliminated* ........................................... 156

**Dissipating Funds during the Divorce** .................................. **157**

**Family Law Appeals** ................................................................. **159**

**What If I'm Not Happy with My Divorce Lawyer?** .................. **161**
*Conclusion* ........................................................................... 165

**Equitable Distribution of Personal-Injury
Employment Discrimination and Workers' Compensation
Awards in New Jersey** ............................................................. **166**

**An Overview of Domestic-Violence Law in New Jersey** ........ **169**
*Confidentiality and Restraining Orders* ............................... 169
*Definition of "Victim" under the Act* ................................... 170
*The Battered-Spouse Defense* .............................................. 170
*Temporary Restraining Orders (TROs)* ................................. 170
*The Domestic-Violence Complaint* ................................. 171
*Discovery at a Final Restraining Order Hearing* ............ 172
*Standard of Review/Standard of Proof* .......................... 172
*Final Restraining Orders* ....................................................... 172
*Appeals of Final Restraining Orders* .............................. 174
*Types of Relief Offered by a Restraining Order* ................... 174
*Marital Torts (Tevis Claims)* .................................................. 175
*Dismissal of Restraining Orders* ........................................... 175
*Civil Restraints* ..................................................................... 176

**Happily Even After** .................................................................. **177**
*What is Happily Even After?* .................................................. 177
*Loose Baggage: Common Post-Divorce Issues* ................... 178
*The Benefits of Working with Your Spouse Post-Divorce* .... 181
*Holiday Parenting Time* .................................................. 181
*Financials* ........................................................................ 181

*Avoiding Outside Intervention*........................................ *182*

*Custody of Pets* ................................................. *182*

*What Can We Learn about Personal Finance*
*from Divorced Couples?* ........................................ *183*

*Be Aware of Your Family's Finances*.................................. *184*

*Work as a Team* ................................................. *185*

*Don't Be Judgmental* ............................................ *186*

*Learn* ...................................................... *187*

*Keep Good Notes and Save Documents*............................. *187*

*Consider Using a Parenting Coordinator Post-Divorce*....... *188*

*A Word on Prenuptial Agreements for Those*
*Who Intend on Remarrying*...................................... *190*

*Should I Sign a Prenup?* ........................................ *192*

**When Your Ex's Baggage Threatens Your Happily *Even* After 195**

*The Impact of Drugs and Mental Health Issues*
*on a Marriage*........................................ *195*

*Pursue Legal Actions while Evidence Is Strongest* .............. *196*

**Post-Divorce Out-of-State Relocation and Removal Law ....... 198**

*Removal Law in New Jersey*.................................... *198*

*After the Divorce: Store Your Important Documents*
*in a Safe Place*........................................ *201*

**Conclusion.......................................................... 204**

**Why Choose Carl Taylor Law, LLC?........................................ 206**

# *Foreword*

**If you're contemplating divorce,** you know a
lot about pain: raw, emotional, gut-wrenching pain. The person
you once stood beside and made promises to is now the one who
no longer wants to live another day with you or the one you can
no longer abide … or both.

When a friend becomes an enemy, when a trusted ally become a betrayer, when love turns to apathy or worse, then your
heart will be crushed and your mind may go into the spin cycle:
"What should I do? Where do I begin? How will I survive? How
will I make it financially? Emotionally? What will become of
my home … my life … my future … my children?"

No one goes into marriage planning for or preparing for
divorce, but when it hits, and it can hit like a hurricane, it can
devastate everyone in its path. As a seasoned therapist who
has worked extensively with divorced and divorcing men and
women and their children, I have had a front row seat to it all.
I've seen lives and hearts scarred beyond recognition, but I've
also seen others recover and rebuild their lives, sometimes even
better than before. And while each situation has its own unique
set of elements and factors, its own nuances, its own story to

be told, everyone, to recover well, will need supportive friends (definitely), a good therapist (probably), and a wise and experienced attorney (absolutely) to guide them along the way.

No one goes into surgery or should go into surgery without being well informed about preoperative care, the surgery itself, and post-operative care. Likewise, no one should go through divorce unprepared and ill informed. In his book *Happily Even After*, family law attorney Carl Taylor has provided a comprehensive guide to the questions you want answered and the questions you didn't even know to ask about divorce in New Jersey. Mr. Taylor provides an invaluable manual to a journey you never intended to walk but has now become (or may become) yours to walk. The book will equip you with technical and legal information, but what makes it unique is that it also addresses emotions—yours, your children's, your partners—a topic most attorneys skittishly avoid.

*Glenn Murphy, LPC*
New Jersey

# *Legal Disclaimers*

**Please note** that this book does not create a legal obligation for you or our firm. This book does not create an attorney-client relationship. This book is for informational purposes only and provides general advice. It cannot and does not supplant actual legal advice. Every case is different, and this book is general in nature. Also, the laws and processes are always changing. If you rely on the information in this book, you do so at your own risk. We expressly waive any liability in regard to this book.

This book provides general information of interest to our clients and prospective clients; it does not constitute legal advice. You should consult with legal counsel to determine how the law may apply to your specific situation. Please also note that each county may have its own court procedures. This book discusses only New Jersey laws and procedures.

# Introduction

**Hello.** If you're reading this, perhaps you or someone you know has issues related to family law. Perhaps you have questions regarding a divorce matter, a custody dispute, a post-judgment issue, or a premarital agreement. If so, please read on to learn about family and divorce law in New Jersey.

I originally created this overview and have updated it to reflect important changes in the law. Through years of family law practice, I've learned that the better informed my clients are, the easier it is for me to assist them through their important legal issues. I wish to work with clients who want to be engaged in the process. Because courts, attorneys, the law itself can be intimidating at first, I hope this information helps make the process less intimidating; that's why I wrote this book.

If you're meeting with an attorney or considering legal representation, there is likely a serious legal issue in your life. You may be confused as to your rights and responsibilities. It's important that you take steps to understand your rights and the legal process. Part of my job as an attorney is to educate my clients so that the laws and court processes are not as daunting as they might otherwise seem. This general overview is a starting point in that education.

I believe that the better informed my clients are, the more efficiently I can provide my services to them and that what they spend in the process will be utilized in the best way for implementing strategies and techniques with the highest return on investment.

I also believe it is beneficial in general and for our state for our citizens getting married, contemplating divorce, or post-divorce to understand the process. The more we can all operate in good faith, the better off we will be.

If you retain or have retained my firm, you will be able to reference this book throughout your case. Any time you can find your answer in the book rather than by calling my office, you're saving yourself money. By better understanding your rights, you can ask me more-specific questions. Of course, if you have any questions, our firm is always available to help you. I encourage my clients to contact me any way they want to; I will do my best to quickly respond.

This book is meant as a supplement to legal representation, but in no way does it replace the need to consider all the fact-specific components that make up each individual's case. Accordingly, the general information provided herein does not constitute specific legal advice.

This book will provide you with a summary of New Jersey divorce and family law. I have attempted to write this not in "legalize" but in a manner easily understood by anyone contemplating a divorce. Although this book cannot constitute legal advice as divorces are so fact-sensitive, it should provide a good overview of the process. I welcome any feedback or criticism so I can improve future editions of this work.

Feel free to read this at your leisure, and don't hesitate to contact my office if you have any questions. Whether you decide to retain my firm or not, I wish you the best of luck with your legal matter.

Very truly yours,
*Carl A. Taylor III, Esq.*
908-237-3096

## CHAPTER 1

# *About Carl A. Taylor III, Esq.*

 **BEFORE YOU READ THIS BOOK,** you're probably interested in my credentials. Don't worry—we'll get to them soon enough. Since we'll spend time together, I wanted to first let you know who I am and where I come from. If you decide to work with our firm someday, I can't wait to learn about your story and to discuss how we can work together to resolve your important family law issues.

When I was a child, my parents had to hire an attorney to confront an issue that was not their fault. Although they were hard working and honest, the case had negative impact on them; I have always believed their lawyer did not properly protect their interests.

The incident made me understand at a young age the importance of the legal system, that it was not always fair, and that the integrity and sophistication of lawyers can make a big difference in the outcome of a legal matter. I decided at a young age to go to law school to fight for those who are unfamiliar with the system and to do so in an efficient, honest, and professional manner.

Nearly a decade later, I was in law school; I was convinced I would sue insurance companies or otherwise work on behalf of those facing a power imbalance. My blue-collar roots were a sizable chip on my shoulder then. I took a family law class on a whim. I was not all that familiar with divorce growing up in an intact family. I was surprised when I enjoyed the course but figured my fondness for it stemmed mostly from the A I received in the class and a good professor.

When I entered law school, the economy was booming. By the time I graduated in 2009, I had student loan debt, was newly married, and the economy had crashed. I had been a solid student, but even top graduates from Rutgers were facing rejections and delays in gaining employment.

Always a hard worker, I mailed out hundreds of resumes including one to every judge in the state seeking a one-year law clerkship (during which I hoped to ride out the recession and gain contacts for long-term employment). The first judge who offered me a job happened to be Judge Picheca, JSC, a family law judge in Somerset County. I accepted the job offer on the spot, and we moved to central New Jersey.

During my clerkship, I saw firsthand that power dynamics and the importance of lawyers in family courts cannot be underestimated. I took an active interest in the family law motions and the important issues of custody, alimony, and the division of assets. Who can have less of a say in a case than a young child whose parents are divorcing or separating? Judge Picheca mentored me not only in the law but also in personal discipline, being practical, and not allowing your ego to interfere with your client's best interests.

Following my clerkship, I worked for a respected family law firm near Princeton, New Jersey. I later partnered in a firm where I served as deputy county counsel for Somerset County for several years. My experience in civil litigation in federal and state courts helps me now in handling complex divorce litigation, but family law remained an active part of my practice even during those years.

In November 2017, nearly a decade after passing the New Jersey bar, and then the father of two daughters, I left the partnership to open Carl Taylor Law, LLC in Hunterdon County. Now, I walk my daughter to the school bus every morning and then go to work, where I lead a team of dedicated staff in working hard for our clients, protecting their rights, and ensuring that all my clients have their say in court and the results they deserved.

When you stop in, we want you to feel welcome and that you are not just a client but part of our team. Indeed, attorneys and clients work closely together in family law matters, and we'll need to rely on each other to obtain the best results.

In Dante's *Inferno*, the deceased poet Virgil acts as a guide for Dante essentially rowing the boat and showing Dante the inner workings of the inferno, purgatory, and eventually ascending to paradise. As a divorce and family law attorney, I relate strongly with Virgil. I am not the hero of the story—you are. It is ultimately your quality of life that is in jeopardy.

However, this is likely your first or second divorce. I have been "divorced" more than a hundred times in terms of the divorce cases I've handled, so like Virgil, though I am not the hero of the tale, I am familiar with the surroundings and want to do everything I can to assist you through what can at times be the hell (or at least the purgatory) of divorce through to *Paradiso.* That's why the tagline of our firm is "Happily *Even* After."

I hope this book will provide you with the information and mind-set necessary to combat whatever divorce and family law issues you are confronting and that you may get to your own Happily *Even* After.

## CARL'S CREDENTIALS

Carl has been quoted in the *New Jersey Law Journal* on the subject of changes to palimony law and has been published multiple times in national family law magazines as well as the *New Jersey Law Journal* on the subject of divorce and family law. He hosts Happily *Even* After, a weekly New Jersey divorce and family law podcast, and he maintains a busy and growing divorce and family law practice in central New Jersey. The firm's website www.mynjdivorcelawyer.com is a great additional resource.

Carl clerked for Judge Picheca, JSC, of the Somerset County Superior Court, Family Division during the 2009–2010 term, and he has actively represented clients in all family law and divorce matters since then seeking to efficiently and fairly represent clients through the difficult transition period of divorce so they can go on to live Happily *Even* After.

Carl volunteers as a Somerset County Early Settlement Panel member and has donated time to domestic-violence education and causes. He also works as the appointed municipal prosecutor in various towns and has an extensive background in civil litigation, something he utilizes for an added edge in high-conflict divorce matters, custody disputes, or other family law litigation.

Carl resides in Hunterdon County, New Jersey, with his wife, two daughters, and an overzealous rough collie (think the opposite of Lassie in every way). In Carl's rare downtime, he enjoys reading presidential biographies and hiking and backpacking, having hiked hundreds of miles of the Appalachian Trail and every mile of the trail in New Jersey.

His firm is engaged in the community and in giving back to Hunterdon County and has an annual scholarship awarded to high school seniors interested in becoming lawyers.

# CHAPTER 2

## *About You*

**If you're reading this book,** it is likely you or someone important to you is considering or already going through a New Jersey divorce, separation, custody dispute, or other important family law issue.

You may feel stuck in a loveless marriage and exhausted by having tried to work things out. You may be in a violent or unsafe situation with a volatile partner. Your spouse may have had an affair, or perhaps you have. It is my belief that the single biggest issue to confront in a divorce is not any legal statute or law, not any complex discovery issue or asset to divide, but rather emotions.

We bring to a divorce a great deal of emotion. Most people getting divorced or contemplating divorce feel a great mixture of emotions. Some clients have described it to me as facing all the stages of grief simultaneously mixed with remnants of love. What could be a more volatile mixture than that?

In a divorce, the partner who is taken by surprise often finds it most difficult to move forward. Sometimes, one party might offer a very fair settlement of the case but the other will not agree. Some people are very stubborn and will not agree out of misguided principles. Others can view divorce as a battleground on which they try to inflict as much harm as possible on the opposing parties, but often, they inflict that pain on themselves in the process. And way too frequently, innocent children are caught in the crossfire.

People going through a divorce sometimes do not understand the nature of their actions because they are too emotionally involved. That is normal, but divorce is not a game and shouldn't be treated as such; it's serious business. Although courtroom procedure and legal minutiae will have to be dealt with, divorces and family law matters are often a highly personal process that will likely have a great impact on people and their children.

Just as your future changed the day you got married, so it will change the day you or your partner file for divorce and again once the divorce is finalized. You may believe your divorce is an interesting wizards' duel of sorts, but what about the collateral damage to yourself and everyone else around you?

Divorce is a time when many people lose their sense of self. Many people lose their jobs during a divorce because it impacts their concentration and takes up a great deal of time. The alternative of a loveless or abusive marriage is of course generally not any better. Understand going in to the divorce that it is a brick-by-brick matter that may take up to a year or more to complete.

If you attempt to be measured in your responses to a divorce that's in the works and work with an attorney who will do the same, you can save yourself a lot of money and a great deal of headaches. Of course, if you're being pushed around and the other side is not acting in good faith, you'll have to be more aggressive to neutralize that.

Our firm assists people like you every day in crafting divorces that will reference your unique future goals. What is your ideal parenting arrangement? What assets will you be entitled to? How can you make sure your prenuptial agreement will be enforced? What amount of alimony and child support should be paid? These are all decisions that will have a long-term impact on your and your children's lives.

As you are reading this book, please take notes as appropriate; feel free to highlight sections, and then come back and reference sections of this book that apply to you and skip over sections that do not. But more than anything else, when you're reading this book and throughout your divorce, write down your ultimate goals and do your best not to lose sight of them.

This book will cover the nuts and bolts of New Jersey divorce procedure, provide a review of relevant New Jersey divorce law, and suggest tips for a successful divorce.

Our firm's tagline, "Happily *Even* After," is a reminder to our clients and our firm that divorce should never be viewed in a vacuum but rather in a global and holistic manner that always maintains a long view toward the future and works toward a breathing document that can address issues as they arise to avoid costly future litigation.

**Write down your ultimate goals and do your best not to lose sight of them.**

In our office, we have a framed picture of two people in a family law courtroom in the 1990s (with lawyers and judges present) dividing what must be about a thousand Beanie Babies. They say a picture tells a thousand words, and the point of that picture should be self-evident. Do the right thing for yourself and your children, hire the right lawyer, keep informed, don't lose sight of your goals, and get to your Happily *Even* After as soon as you can.

Divorce can be hell, but it doesn't have to be. We'll steer you onto the right path, help you formulate plans and goals, and lead you to your personal Happily *Even* After.

# CHAPTER 3

# Firm Mission Statement: Sharks and Dolphins

Recently, one of my clients left a five-star positive Google review that contained the following language among general praise: "If you are looking for an amoral shark to punish your not-yet ex for sins both real and imagined, this isn't the law firm for you, but I strongly recommend Carl Taylor Law to everyone else."

I went home that evening and read those lines over and over. I read them to my wife and asked her input. Although it was a positive review, I was concerned because lawyers of course have large egos and I am no exception. I want to be moral, but I also want to be a shark or at least thought of as one should that ever becomes necessary. Hey, I'd settle for being considered an agitated stringray depending on the day. Moreover, it's what many clients expect and even demand. They're paying good money, and they want a shark.

Somehow, despite my being personally stubborn, occasionally ill tempered, and when appropriate quite aggressive, this review was similar to other feedback I have received throughout my career. Often, that feedback has been positive: "You were a pleasure to work with," clients may say. Or "You were tough when necessary, but I appreciate your being logical and having a steady hand during my divorce case." Other times, the comments have been a bit more pointed: "You *do* have it in you to be a real mean bastard, right?" at least three clients have asked me over the years in one form or another.

Many lawyers bill themselves as sharks. Despite my good success throughout my career and extensive litigation experience including winning cases in state, appellate, and federal courts, certain clients simply do not see me as a shark. I wondered if I was too down to earth given my blue-collar background. Being an average Joe is something I pride myself on, but I and others see TV ads for slick, fast-talking attorneys wearing thousand-dollar suits. I considered perhaps changing my approach and becoming more aggressive so I'd be perceived as more aggressive; I thought that through and had an epiphany: in a divorce, clients think they need a shark, but often, what they need is a dolphin.

It's said that dolphins can act as life rafts and help distressed humans back to shore. Moreover, it is said that dolphins *can* effectively fight and often defeat sharks when necessary. Although dolphins may not go looking for unnecessary fights and may favor efficiency, when the stakes are high, dolphins do what's necessary. Sharks may be indiscriminate about what they eat, but dolphins are calculated and precise. Sharks may eat their own, but dolphins don't.

Clients **think** they need a shark, but often, what they **need** is a dolphin.

I realized that as a lawyer, I might be more of a dolphin than a shark, and I further realized that that was more than okay. Besides, I am who I am. I can no more will myself to be a metaphorical shark that a real dolphin could will itself to become a shark.

## CHAPTER 4

# *New Jersey Divorce and Family Law*

**Family law attorneys** may be the only type of lawyers who need to keep tissues in their conference room. Many clients are sad about their divorces or custody situations, others are angry, and many are a mixture of such negative emotions. There are exceptions of course, but that's the general rule.

They say divorce is worse than suffering the death of a loved one and it's therefore only logical that a party's emotions can sometimes take the reins of a divorce. Emotions are not something often spoken about in law school. Budding attorneys may hear about "emotional distress" as a type of claim in torts class, but dealing with clients' strong emotions is rarely if ever addressed.

As I often advise clients, the law is callous. It doesn't always make sense and is not always just, but for better or sometimes worse, it does its best to utilize logic and reason rather than emotion. This leads to a situation in family law in which occasionally even judges are at a loss about how to proceed given the level of emotion that can come up in a case. Duels remain illegal as of this writing, so ultimately, there's nothing a judge can order that will make up for how hurt or angry a divorcing party may feel at his or her ex.

I mentioned before the photo I have in my office of a couple in the 1990s dividing a Beanie Baby collection in court under the assistance of a judge and with lawyers present. The point is simple: try to focus on the important issues. Paying me to fight for a share of a pension or for fair custody makes sense, but fighting over a jar of change does not. My background in civil litigation taught me to view every case through a cost-benefit analysis. My clients and I need to consider the cost of my services, the cost of expert witnesses if necessary, and the likelihood of success for a given course of action to determine if the return on investment is worth it.

This is the way large, sophisticated clients such as insurance companies, banks, and governmental entities view litigation. I know that because I've worked with such clients. But it's often not the way people who are unfamiliar with litigation think—not when their minds are clouded with emotions. Those seeking a divorce may find it hard to hold onto a sense of balance and perspective. The result could be a delayed divorce proceeding, hard feelings that may negatively impact their children, less personal satisfaction, and ultimately a much smaller pie to carve up.

**Try to focus on the important issues.**

Some people want to play games, but divorce is definitely not a game; it's serious business with serious consequences and real risks. You can get even or you can get to your Happily *Even* After.

## EFFICIENT SOLUTIONS

At Carl Taylor Law, LLC, our mission is to work with you from the initial consultation toward ambitious but reasonable goals all the way to the end of litigation. Like a college counselor, we'll be honest with you if a particular desire or outcome is a stretch.

Though most people would love to go to an Ivy League school, not everyone has a realistic chance of doing so. If something is unattainable, we'll do our best to tell you before you spend money and time on a losing proposition. Seeking ambitious or realistic results can be the difference between wasting time and money and moving the matter forward in an efficient manner.

I'll tell you upfront that while we may not be sharks, we'll be honest with you and embody the spirit of the dolphin. Not every attorney has that attitude and that belief system, but we do.

Regardless of the path you choose, I hope this book will present potential paths and provide you with knowledge that will assist you in your important divorce or family law matter.

## CHAPTER 5

# *Seven Simple Steps to Take before Filing a Divorce…*
# *And Ten Things That Might Surprise You about Divorce in New Jersey*

## SEVEN SIMPLE STEPS TO TAKE BEFORE FILING A DIVORCE …

If you're reading this book, I'm guessing you or someone you know is contemplating a New Jersey divorce. You may have important questions that need to be answered such as,

- Should I leave or stay in the marital residence?
- How is custody addressed in the interim?
- How are assets divided?
- What can I do to make sure my spouse doesn't waste marital funds?
- How does the court system work?
- How do I find a qualified New Jersey divorce lawyer?

Through my years of family law practice, I've learned that the better informed my clients are, the easier it is for me to assist them through their important and unique legal issues. Courts, attorneys, the law itself—these things can be intimidating at first. I hope this book helps make the process less so.

It's important that you take steps to understand your rights and the legal process for obtaining them. Divorce will most likely affect your finances, lifestyle, and most important—your children. If you move in an informed manner and with the right lawyer through the process, that can have a huge impact on the outcome and on your life.

Sometimes in tough cases, particularly when my clients start to deviate from my advice, I think of the scene in the great movie *Jerry Maguire* in which sports agent Jerry Maguire asks his football star client Rod Tidwell over and over, "Help me help you." I can relate to that.

In one sense, an attorney-client relationship is similar to a doctor-patient relationship in that the client or patient must take an active role in obtaining the results they desire. A doctor can advise a patient with high blood pressure to watch his or her sodium intake, but it's the patient's responsibility to eat more celery and less fast food. (I know, I know, I'm working on it ...)

## 1. KEEP A JOURNAL/LOG

In family law matters, an almost unlimited number of issues can arise. Keep a log of when alimony checks are sent or received and when you or your spouse takes care of the kids. Note particularly if your spouse was late to pick up the kids or was a no-show and all other important facts and events as your divorce is proceeding. Accurate logs can help clients keep track of their cases' progress, and they can also prove to be important evidence that can help their cases.

## 2. DON'T LOSE YOUR TEMPER

As the old courthouse wisdom goes, lose your temper, lose your case. Text messages, phone conversations, and emails are often used in court to demonstrate domestic violence, lack of fitness of a parent, and many other issues. What may seem like blowing off steam in the heat of the moment may later be taken out of context or used to demonstrate a pattern of such behavior. Anger may also hurt your odds of quickly settling a case and will impact your ability to focus on and achieve your goals.

## 3. CONSIDER MEETING WITH A MENTAL HEALTH EXPERT

People going through divorce are often helped by meeting with a mental health professional. The saying that a divorce is worse than a death in the family is very accurate according to most of my clients. Having a mental health professional in your corner can help alleviate some of the stress or even simply provide coaching to unlock post-divorce goals.

## 4. BE VERY CAREFUL WHEN USING SOCIAL MEDIA

Do not post pictures on Facebook of you out partying or tweet about it while engaged in a contested custody dispute because such pictures may come back to haunt you. Many things can be taken out of context, and it's a lot easier for others to access your social media information than you might expect.

Also note that you might not be allowed to delete what you've posted on social media once a divorce suit is filed; doing so could make it look like you're spoiling potential evidence, so you could be ordered not to do so. Modify your social media presence before filing for divorce. Reputation and credibility are so important in family law cases, and spoliation of evidence rules can make removing or changing posts and pictures on social media look suspicious.

I can't count how many times our firm has been able to attach social media postings by the other side and gain an advantage in the courtroom. You live by the sword and die by the sword in our interconnected world. Being careful about such matters can increase your chances of achieving what you want from a divorce.

## 5. TAKE NOTES AND STORE DOCUMENTS IN A SAFE LOCATION

When you speak with your attorney or something important occurs in your case, make a note of it. Ideally, you should maintain a notebook or a binder of all important documents and information relating to your case. We often give our clients binders for just that purpose, and we tell them to keep it in a secure and private place along with that journal or log I mentioned earlier.

## 6. GET YOUR FINANCES IN ORDER

Make a list of all bank account numbers, maintain copies of you most recent statements, write down important online banking login names and passwords, and otherwise fully understand the marital assets and debts prior to filing for divorce. That will help you should your spouse attempt to dissipate marital funds.

Likewise, do not commingle nonmarital funds such as gifts, inheritances, or personal-injury settlement money particularly if you're considering divorce as such actions may convert such exempt funds into joint marital funds.

## 7. DON'T BE AFRAID TO ASK YOUR ATTORNEY QUESTIONS

You hired an attorney in part to have someone available to answer all your questions. We at Carl Taylor Law encourage our clients to have open dialogue with their lawyers so that they're on the same page and can obtain the best results relating to your specific priorities.

There are many more ways clients can help reduce the costs of litigation, strengthen their cases, and help themselves achieve better results in their cases. When dealing with the court system, things can sometimes feel a little outside a client's control, but focusing on what can be controlled or affected can help attorney and client achieve a successful outcome to the case.

My bonus tip is to learn as much as you can about the divorce process from the right sources. Google is a great place to find basic information, but laws are state specific and they're always changing, so don't rely solely on that.

I know you're the type of person who wants to be informed; that's why you're reading this book. Your commitment to that will pay dividends for you and your children throughout and after the divorce process.

## … AND TEN THINGS THAT MAY SURPRISE YOU ABOUT A NEW JERSEY DIVORCE

Every divorce case is fact sensitive and people sensitive. I often joke that though I've been "divorced" on behalf of my clients over a hundred times, even I always find something unique about each case I've handled.

There are certain surprises, however, that are much more common. The following list will help take some of the guesswork out of your divorce.

### 1. FAULT ISN'T THAT IMPORTANT

You may be shocked to learn that "marital fault" is often unimportant in terms of dividing marital assets or even with issues regarding parenting time. For instance, if one party committed adultery, it's generally not going to make much of a difference in the divorce negotiations or to a family court judge provided that the affair doesn't in some way negatively affect the children.

**Learn as much as you can about the divorce process from the right sources.**

Examples to the contrary, however, include one of the divorcing parties getting involved with someone with a criminal background or a history or drug, alcohol, or child abuse.

### 2. THE LAWS ARE (ESSENTIALLY) GENDER NEUTRAL

If the breadwinner of the family is the woman, she will likely have to pay alimony provided that the laws are properly followed. As for parenting time, the biggest factors will be past history of care for the children, not whether you're their mother or father. Gender neutrality is becoming more the norm—not just in theory but in practice—in today's courtrooms.

### 3. THERE'S PROBABLY NOT A CONSPIRACY

I've had a lot of clients tell me that their exes were well connected and probably getting special treatment from a court, or that they think a certain judge favors men or women. In reality, based on my experience, I'll tell you that that's very rare if nonexistent. I don't mean that people are always treated fairly or that the proper decisions are always rendered, but I'll say that the reasons behind such issues are almost certainly not nefarious.

### 4. THE JUDGE LIKELY WON'T SPEAK WITH YOUR CHILDREN

If you're involved in a custody issue concerning a child or children under age thirteen, few if any judges will be willing to hear their custody preferences even off the record. This issue is up to the discretion of the judges, however. They might want to listen to children ages fourteen to eighteen about custody matters, but most judges prefer to keep children out of the courtroom.

### 5. YOU CAN SUE OR BE SUED FOR A MARITAL TORT

Based on *Tevis v. Tevis*, New Jersey courts recognize "marital torts"; you can sue for personal injuries whether they're physical or emotional as part of a divorce complaint. The process is similar to suing someone for other forms of personal injury such as those someone might suffer in a traffic accident.

## 6. CHILDREN MAY NOT BE EMANCIPATED AT AGE EIGHTEEN OR EVEN TWENTY-ONE

The basic New Jersey standard for considering children emancipated from their parents is whether they have moved beyond the sphere and influence of their parents. Unlike in Pennsylvania, in New Jersey, parents might be required to pay for college and even graduate school for their children along with basic child support and other expenses. This is a fact-sensitive inquiry. Although there is a presumption of independence or emancipation at age eighteen (or graduation from high school), that's rarely enforced unless a child is truly on his or her own and isn't attending additional schooling.

## 7. LAWYERS CANNOT REPRESENT BOTH PARTIES

Sometimes, a prospective client will call me up and ask if I'd draft a settlement agreement for a divorce. They want me to codify what both parties wish for in their divorce or have both parties come in to meet with me. This presents a conflict of interest—and I won't do it. I will represent only one party and recommend that each party gets his or her own independent legal advice.

## 8. GRANDPARENTS WILL OFTEN HAVE NO RIGHTS OF VISITATION WITHOUT A COURT ORDER—AND THAT WILL BE DIFFICULT TO OBTAIN

Parents' rights to parent their children will supersede any rights grandparents think they have to visitation with their grandchildren.

## 9. DIVORCES CAN TAKE MORE THAN A YEAR

Complicated or contested divorces can easily take one or more years; that's the rule, not the exception. That is another reason it's important for you to negotiate in good faith. If both parties agree to the divorce terms, a divorce might be granted in a matter of weeks rather than years.

## 10. PRENUPTIAL AGREEMENTS ARE BECOMING MORE COMMON

Today, a lot of my clients and prospective clients ask about prenuptial agreements, which are no longer solely in the purview of movie stars, tycoons, and celebrities. Prenuptial agreements will continue to become more common for everyone contemplating marriage. Keep in mind, however, that prenuptial agreements will often be challenged as part of the divorce process.

# CHAPTER 6

---

## *The Heart of the Matter— Addressing the Emotional Side of a Divorce*

### BALANCING EMOTION WITH PROPER BOUNDARIES CAN LEAD TO THE OPTIMUM OUTCOME

It may seem a bit odd to cover the topic of emotions in a book focusing on divorce. You might be wondering if I'm some hippie giving you a lecture about feelings. I'm no expert in psychology; my only advanced degree is my law degree. But I believe that in some ways, nobody knows more about the emotions that can be involved in a divorce than divorce lawyers—not in a clinical or expert sense but in a commonsense manner.

When I was a child, my parents would read me a Little Golden Book, *Mr. Bell's Fixit Shop*. Mr. Bell ran a type of hardware store, and he'd say he could "fix anything but a broken heart." In the story, a child becomes heartbroken when her favorite stuffed animal is damaged. But good old Mr. Bell fixes it for her and learns that sometimes, good old craftsmanship can mend even a broken heart.

So though I may seem as likely a candidate as Mr. Bell was on the subject of the heart and have just as much formal training as he did, even a cynical divorce attorney like me starts to see certain patterns. I am much more aggressive now in suggesting that my clients seek individual therapy during a divorce. A divorce—and particularly a contested one—is a marathon, not a sprint. You'll need to stay focused on your goals. You'll need to keep negative emotions such as fear and anger at bay. You'll need to eat right and essentially train as if you're about to run an emotional marathon.

I became a hermit when I was studying for the bar exam, but I took time to exercise every day and eat purportedly brain-healthy foods including blueberries and salmon. I'll tell you that self-control, healthy eating habits, and regular exercise are not my default settings, but I knew back then that I'd need all my energy—brainpower included—to make sure I passed the bar exam.

Any time I spent worrying about my student loans or a negative outcome was time I wouldn't get to spend focusing on my single-minded goal: passing that bar exam on the first try. Luckily, my hard work paid off. Other people—and some of them were smarter than me—failed on their first tries. In certain instances, I'm sure that was because stress had gotten to them.

Why are some quarterbacks with less natural talent better in big games? What was it in a quarterback such as Nick Foles that allowed him to step up and defeat Tom Brady and his Patriots and win the Super Bowl? I'm sure that it was his great concentration on his goals, solid control of his emotions, and not letting negative emotions such as fear get to him. When he threw an interception in the Super Bowl game, he shrugged it off and came back firing until the game was over and he had achieved what appeared to have been the impossible.

In your divorce, you'll go through down moments for which you'll need a strong support network. Because you're reading this book, that means you're already in a good head space—you realize that knowledge can help you overcome stressful, scary situations. The more you know about the risks you face and your rights and responsibilities during a divorce, the more you can maximize the outcome you desire. If meditation is your thing, make sure you stick with it. If you're a runner, keep running. If you're seeing a therapist, keep doing so. And if you think you're alone, remember that almost everyone going through a divorce has had similar thoughts.

As I mentioned, there's a reason people say divorce is worse than a death in the family. It's not easy to always do so, but if you can control your negative emotions and stay positive, you'll have a much better chance of achieving the results you want. In divorces, it's often the case that the only thing you have complete control over is how you respond to what happens. Keep in mind that your divorce will ultimately be finalized and then you can start your Happily *Even* After.

Before we dive deeper into the emotion of a divorce, let's review some of the frequently asked questions I hear as a divorce lawyer.

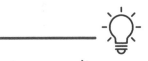

In your divorce, you'll go through down moments for which you'll need a strong support network.

# CHAPTER 7

## *Divorce FAQs*

**Although every case is fact-sensitive,** this section of the book addresses certain issues that often come up at divorce consults.

### Q. HOW LONG WILL IT TAKE TO BE DIVORCED?

**A.** Perhaps surprisingly, this is the number-one question I am asked even before the question of how much a divorce will likely cost.

The average divorce takes about a year. Some take only one or two months while others that are highly contested can drag on for three to even four years. Many factors affect how long it takes to finalize a divorce including whether the parties pursue mediation or litigation, the complexity of the case, the reasonableness of the parties and counsel in negotiations, and the desire of both parties to bring the matter to a close.

## Q. WHAT ARE THE LEGAL FEES INVOLVED IN GETTING DIVORCED?

**A.** As do most New Jersey divorce attorneys, I bill by the hour. For the reasons mentioned above, it is therefore impossible to provide clients with a cost as it will depend on how long it takes to get a divorce decree and more specifically the number of hours of legal work performed.

The cost can therefore range from the low four to the low six figures, though the range for most divorces is more likely between $5,000 and $25,000. I endeavor to work efficiently for my clients to provide encompassing advice while avoiding overly burdensome costs. Generally, I'll ask at least a $5,000 retainer for a contested divorce, less for motions or uncontested divorces.

## Q. WHAT ARE MY RESPONSIBILITIES WHILE THE DIVORCE IS PENDING?

**A.** Essentially, while the divorce is pending (known as the *pendente lite* phase of litigation), both parties are required to maintain the "marital status quo." This means keeping insurance premiums paid, not encumbering or dissipating marital assets or incurring inappropriate marital debt, paying certain regular expenses, and the like. Parenting time and access to children should also maintain the status quo of the marriage.

## Q. WHAT IF SOMEONE COMMITS AN ACT OF DOMESTIC VIOLENCE?

**A.** The victim should immediately contact the police and then the court to file a temporary restraining order.

## Q. WILL I BE ENTITLED TO CUSTODY AND PARENTING TIME?

**A.** In most instances, courts favor joint legal custody, and there is even a move toward joint physical custody. Joint legal custody involves the ability to make important decisions for children while in a child's life while physical custody addresses who will more often be providing daily care to the children. These cases are particularly fact sensitive, but courts almost always favor parenting time for both parents unless that wouldn't be in the best interests of the children.

## Q. HOW IS CHILD SUPPORT CALCULATED?

**A.** New Jersey utilizes Child Support Guidelines, a formula that calls for a weekly child-support obligation based on various factors including all the sources of income (imputed or real) of the parties, the amount of overnights each parent exercises with the children, the number of children, and the children's ages.

## Q. HOW WILL I KNOW IF I'M ENTITLED TO ALIMONY OR IF I HAVE TO PAY ALIMONY?

**A.** Unlike with child support, New Jersey has yet to enact alimony guidelines, though pending legislation could change that. Accordingly, the court addresses a number of factors such as the length of the marriage, the income potential of each party, the parties' ages, and the like in determining whether alimony is appropriate and if so whether it should be permanent, term, rehabilitative, or reimbursement. As stated above, alimony may also be provided *pendente lite*.

## Q. WHY SHOULD I CHOOSE CARL TAYLOR LAW, LLC FOR MY DIVORCE?

**A.** Because we will work with you to assess your goals and help provide closure so you can move on with your life. I hope this book will help you decide if we're a good fit for you and your important New Jersey family law matters.

## Q. WHAT SHOULD I BRING TO AN INITIAL CONSULTATION ABOUT A DIVORCE?

**A.** Our firm has intake procedures and forms even prior to an initial consultation. The more information we have prior to then, the better prepared we'll be to provide preliminary advice on how to proceed.

Though I'm not formally retained as a client's lawyer until a retainer agreement is signed by both parties, I like to provide my clients with general and some specific information on a number of topics including likely alimony and child-support ranges. I often email intake forms to prospective clients, and they are also available for downloading from our firm's website so they can be filled out prior to an initial consultation.

I encourage prospective clients to provide the filled-out intake form, tax returns, prior court orders, and any other relevant documents prior to the initial consultation. If that's not possible, I spend time going over that information at the initial consultation.

## Q. WHAT WILL YOU ASK ME DURING THE INITIAL DIVORCE CONSULTATION?

**A.** Just as with your first meeting with a doctor, I like to begin with basic information such as prospective clients' contact information, date of birth, date of marriage, and so on—the basics. Then generally, I ask prospective clients why they are meeting with me. It's important that we air out the marital issues so we can later focus on gather more-technical information. Has the prospective client attempted marriage counseling? Is their marriage salvageable? Has his or her spouse already retained an attorney or filed formal divorce proceedings?

From there, I will generally ask a series of questions in hopes of learning the parties' financial situation. New Jersey is a no-fault divorce state, so financial considerations along with child-custody issues are at the heart of New Jersey divorce law. Some of the areas I will address with a client include these.

- both parties' income/employment
- the children's situations
- possible custody issues
- real property such as the marital home
- bank, investment, and retirement accounts and pensions
- estimated college costs
- premarital, gifted, personal injury, or inherited property
- life and health insurance policies
- automobiles, vehicles, boats
- stock options
- businesses
- profit-sharing plans
- loans and debts

Once these and other important topics are discussed, I provide potential clients with some perspective on where their cases may be heading. I discuss alternate dispute-resolution options with them. If litigation seems likely, I provide some insight into how the case will likely turn out. I will also point prospective clients to my New Jersey Divorce Overview (available for free on our website, mynjdivorcelawyer.com), which also explains the process.

Initial consultations end with a question-and-answer session and information on the next steps if a prospective client wishes to become a client; this includes likely costs, our fees, and the retainer amount.

## A NOTE ON NEW JERSEY DIVORCE: INITIAL CONSULTATION

A divorce initial consultation is very important as it's the first time a prospective attorney and client meet. If both parties are prepared for the meeting, that can help them decide whether to start a successful working relationship.

## FAQ CONCLUSION

Some clients find the initial consultation stressful, so I wanted to address the nature of an initial consultation, at least how our firm handles them.

By focusing on the goals of the client and meshing them with the facts of the case and the relevant law, a client and I can tailor a specific strategy early on that will guide us to the desired outcome.

# CHAPTER 8

# What if I'm Not Ready to Get Divorced Yet?

**When people first visit** our office as prospective clients, they're not always ready to file for divorce; they might simply be searching for information because they want to know their options. Others are ready to file immediately, and some have already filed without an attorney and want to hire a lawyer.

Sometimes, I meet with people who are dissatisfied with their current lawyers. Many people are in therapy and hoping it will work out but want to explore the process in case it doesn't. Some may not outright admit it but perhaps they are looking to craft a divorce plan and see what they can do now to improve their situation should they need to file in the future. Others are willing to consider mediation or other more-amicable forms of divorce.

Some want to have a legal separation, and I explain to them that there's no such thing in New Jersey; "divorce from bed and board" is the closest thing we have to a legal separation.

Other prospective clients have tried mediation and have a nonbinding memorandum of understanding that they wish to finalize. Some have Divorce Agreements their spouses have proposed that they want me to review. Some have gotten divorced and remarried to the same person and want to divorce again.

## SAVING THE MARRIAGE … OR NOT

So what's the point of the somewhat long-winded list above? Simply this: to let anyone reading this and contemplating divorce know that it's okay if you're not ready to file for divorce. It's okay if your goal is to save your marriage, and it's okay if you feel conflicted about it—it would be unusual not to.

Learning about a possible course of action doesn't mean you're going to proceed with it. I've read many books about creating a suburban homestead, but if you came to my house today, you'd still find only a patch of discolored carrots and a lazy collie that hasn't herded anything besides children.

Few people enter a marriage without a lot of thought, and likewise, few leave a marriage without considering the ramifications. There are bills to be paid, children to be raised, and assets to divide. Beyond that are emotions—sometimes intense emotions—to resolve. There may be feelings of loss, betrayal, and guilt.

Simply talking to a divorce attorney doesn't mean you're ready to proceed with a divorce just as reading this book doesn't mean you need or want to file for divorce. I meet certain clients who I think should divorce, but I always keep in mind that that's not my decision to make; only they can and should make that decision.

So if you're contemplating a divorce but uncertain how to proceed, keep in mind that that's okay. If you've met with an attorney months ago and now wish to proceed, there's no need to feel embarrassed about returning to that attorney if you feel you're now ready. Divorce lawyers are used to meeting with people and retaining some on the spot, not hearing back from others for months and even years until they're ready, and not hearing from others ever again. That's normal and okay.

So if you're not ready to move forward yet, that's perfectly normal. If you're on the fence, perhaps this book will give you some clarity on your situation that will help you decide one way or another.

## SHOULD I DISCUSS MY DESIRE TO DIVORCE WITH MY SPOUSE?

A divorce filing or informal separation doesn't mean life suddenly ceases. As I mentioned above, there are still bills to be paid, friends to see, children to raise, and yes, soon-to-be exes to deal with. As a divorce attorney, I've found that in some instances, divorcing couples communicate more during their divorce than during their marriage.

Of course the communication is not always healthy or productive, but sometimes it is. I've heard from clients that their spouses had negative opinions about me, but then, I'd had some clients who worked out better results with their spouses than I or any court could have provided because they sat down and talked with each other.

I advise my clients, "I know the law, but you know your spouse." I say that because emotions can play a far more important role in divorces than reason does. For that reason—except in abuse situations or when a restraining order is in effect—I often tell clients that it would be best if they communicated with their spouses by themselves.

I also advise clients not to put anything in writing even if it's unlikely to be binding when represented by counsel and not to make any guarantees, but I encourage them to talk as part of a settlement negotiation, which will be confidential under court rules. I also advise them against giving away any trial strategy and to cease communicating if the situation becomes tense.

However, in certain cases where there isn't much animosity, clearing the air and attempting to discuss amicable resolutions without lawyers or mediators hanging around can be beneficial. That's because some emotions simply need to run their course. I've been in mediation and settlement conferences with clients that seemed a waste of time one day but then work out the next day after matters were aired and a former emotionally charged atmosphere calmed down.

Based on my experiences with clients, I think that the seven stages of grieving psychologists talk about are true. Many clients ask me at the start, "How long will it take to get divorced?" and I advise them that the answer is when a judge issues an opinion following a divorce trial, shortly after all negative emotions are properly drained, or whenever reason sets in—whichever comes first.

Sometimes, I'll ask clients who view divorce as combat, "Do you want to pay for my kids' college or your own?" That's a polite but direct way to let them know they're pushing too hard and are unnecessarily upping the time and the money it'll take them to finalize their divorces.

I've been noticing more and more even among attorneys the attitude or stated opinion that divorce is a game with winners and losers, but that attitude doesn't serve anyone well. I think of divorce as a process of creating a rulebook or drawing up a contract. A marriage is a contract but absent a prenup, it's one with vague terms.

Good divorce lawyers should be able to guide their clients through divorce by creating fair and simply stated terms so they can go through the process following some fair rules and get on with their lives with the least emotional baggage as possible. I have found that that can cut down on the cost of a divorce and reduce the chances of having to jump back in and go through post-divorce litigation, which can cost as much as the divorce itself. That's why I encourage my clients to talk with their spouses and get their issues—in some cases the real issues that are in their subconscious—out on the table. That can provide clarity to both parties and calm down angry attitudes.

So back to the question "Should I discuss my divorce with my spouse?" the simple answer is that in many instances it can be effective provided that certain parameters are in place. That way, when attorneys or mediators get involved, all parties can hopefully limit the issues and save litigation costs.

## TO WHAT EXTENT SHOULD EMOTION FUEL A DIVORCE?

An old lawyer joke is that criminal lawyers generally deal with bad people acting their best and divorce lawyers generally deal with good people acting their worst. Emotion is an inescapable part of a divorce. Ultimately, nobody gets married expecting to be divorced, and there are many feelings and emotions involved in a divorce, which by its very nature is an *ending* and perhaps even an admission of failure.

In my years of practice, I've seen lawyers stoke the fires of anger and resentment to make a case more litigious and thus more expensive. It's rare, but I've seen it. I've also had clients whose emotions likely ruined their chances of achieving a positive outcome. I've tried to limit such situations, but I can help only those clients who want to or can help themselves—the Jerry Maguire attitude I mentioned earlier.

I've had clients tell me that they had at times been unhappy with my lack of emotion during a divorce but later thanked me for having moved their cases forward; they came to see the value in a more stoic and rational approach. And most judges don't like blowhards. My goal in most litigation and particularly with divorces is to appear to be the most sane and logical person in the room. I encourage my clients to seek counseling so they can control their emotions and follow suit in that matter; that can help result in a better outcome.

If you can take out the emotional factors, divorces can be fairly simple and straightforward. New Jersey law generally recommends a near fifty-fifty split of marital assets, and in general, divorce lawyers know the existing standards for alimony and child support. Custody and parenting-time schedules are often best worked out between the parties themselves.

What can make family law cases difficult is the need to get four people—the spouses and their lawyers—on the same page. If even one of them doesn't want to settle the issues involved, wants to drag it out, is looking for revenge, and so on, that can draw out a divorce that could otherwise have been resolved much quicker.

I always consider divorce in terms of risks versus rewards; I advise my clients to do a cost-benefit analysis in terms of the money and emotional energy they want to spend and what they hope to achieve. That can keep a divorce from becoming a Wild West shoot out, and that benefits everyone. I also advise my clients not to make mountains out of molehills and not to think two wrongs make a right; such thinking comes with a high price in terms of money, time, and emotional upheaval and leaves a client wondering, *Was that all worth it?*

That's why I encourage my clients to communicate with their spouses. Mediation and collaborative law can help turn the down the heat in contentious times. Collaborative law is an alternative dispute-resolution method that largely takes the divorce out of the court system. It's basically mediation with more structure and involvement by counsel. In a collaborative divorce, both parties and their attorneys agree to amicably work out the divorce and freely share financial and other information; consider it divorce by agreement rather than by litigious disagreement.

Emotions will always play a role in a divorce; I've never represented a robot (although in the future, who knows?), but I do know that controlling emotions can keep a divorce from becoming a battle in which everyone loses.

## ... BUT DON'T BE A PUSHOVER

To balance some of my advice on the importance of being reasonable, I'll point out that I always suggest that clients set proper boundaries and not become pushovers or accept bad deals. Too often, people come into a divorce too angry or too tired or guilty or whatever to properly negotiate for what's fair. Being level headed and between those extremes is the sweet spot for an optimal divorce settlement.

Guilty feelings can be some of the most troublesome emotions in a divorce. Just because you had an affair doesn't mean you shouldn't be allowed to retire someday. That is not the way the law views it. Indeed, in most instances, New Jersey law takes no position regarding who has the moral high ground in a divorce.

Divorce can be a marathon. Too often, people get worn down too quickly by the process and end up agreeing to terms they later regret. That's why focus and taking care of yourself are so important during a divorce. You need to be able to put that oxygen mask over your own face first before you can help others such as your children.

What I mean by saying you shouldn't be a pushover is this: if your spouse has a long-term and serious drug problem, you should fight against his or her having unsupervised parenting time. And if you believe your spouse has stashed thousands in cash in a safety deposit box or in cryptocurrencies (more on that later), you'll need an expert to take aggressive steps to find out if that's true. There's a difference between being reasonable and being a pushover. Your divorce lawyer can help you understand when you're being reasonable and when you're giving in too much.

Your children will need you to be strong for them. They are not a party to a divorce, but nobody will likely be impacted more than they will be. The way you handle your divorce will have a big effect on their present and future.

You'll get tired during the process, but so will the other side. To some extent, that can prompt both parties to reach a settlement. But if you start just going through the motions or stop caring, consider taking some time—maybe a long weekend or whatever it takes—to make sure you're not making decisions that you'll live to regret such as waiving your right to alimony, accepting less child support than your children are entitled to, giving up custody or parenting time you're entitled to, or waiving your spouse's requirement to contribute to your children's college costs.

So be reasonable, but don't be a pushover.

## A WORD ON RECONCILIATION

One lesson I've learned the hard way is never to bash the ex-boyfriend or ex-girlfriend of a friend or family member. I've seen too many examples of on-again, off-again, and then on-again relationships to give my opinions of anybody's ex. The next thing you know, they've reconciled and you end up the pariah.

That's why I always ask my divorce clients about the possibility of reconciliation. I'll ask them questions to get a general sense of their marriages and the reasons behind their breakdown. I want to find out if there's a possibility for reconciliation, and I'll recommend marriage or couple's therapy to see if the marriage can be salvaged. The divorce process can be difficult and expensive, and it should generally not be commenced unless the client is close to 100 percent certain that there's no reasonable prospect of reconciliation.

At uncontested-divorce hearings, judges and lawyers will often ask the parties about the possibility of reconciliation. The state's interest in

Your children will need you to be strong for them. They are not a party to a divorce, but nobody will likely be impacted more than they will be.

preserving a marriage is not as strong as it once was, but it's still there.

Many times, emotions provide a framework for divorce proceedings. People are uncertain about how they really feel; they have conflicting thoughts and emotions. I've learned that some people can love their spouses but still want to divorce them. Some people remain in loveless marriages while others for a variety of reasons want to leave loving marriages. Many times, people aren't sure if they want to try to work things out, separate, or divorce. Until that issue is resolved, in many cases, it might not make sense for someone to proceed with any legal divorce proceedings. I've witnessed couples reconciling even after filing for divorce, and I was happy for that. I just wish they'd reached that point prior to paying all the costs—emotional as well as financial—up to that point.

So if you're unsure of whether you want to divorce, meet with a divorce attorney for at least an initial consultation. Engage in some through soul searching and try to find out if you want to try to salvage your marriage; that could be time very well spent.

## ENDINGS ARE IMPORTANT IN NEW JERSEY DIVORCE LAW

We often judge movies by their endings or our favorite teams' scores at the end of a game. In the film *The Dark Night*, someone said we "either die a hero or live long enough to be the villain." Likewise, in a divorce, attorneys and their clients often focus on the outcome of a case. Who received custody of the children? How much or how little alimony will be paid? Which parents is entitled to parenting time during Christmas this year? What is lost in this somewhat myopic view is the importance of another ending—the end of a relationship. So much of a New Jersey divorce outcome is decided by the timing of a divorce.

Alimony statutes take a more global view, but generally, only the last five years of a marriage in terms of finances will be considered. If you file for divorce when your spouse's income is at an all-time low, that could affect the alimony you might receive. Divorce in New Jersey takes into consideration overtime and bonuses. Sometimes, an individual's recent success can end up harming the outcome of their case. Likewise, a relationship's current status quo is important in regard to custody and parenting time.

I'm not suggesting that people should try to game the system, neglect maintaining the status quo, or start turning down all overtime if they feel separation or divorce is imminent because such divorce "planning" can be detrimental to a case and in some instances—particularly involving hiding assets—may even be illegal. Rather, I want show how the timing of a relationship's ending can be just as important as the ending achieved by divorce and a marital settlement. This is because the facts associated with a relationship's ending (particularly when a formal divorce pleading is filed) may affect more than any other single factor the ultimate disposition of a case.

My basic questions include these: Is this a fair result? If one person has been working eighty hours a week while the other was working only part time though that person could easily have been working much more or is sitting around waiting on an inheritance, should alimony be based on just their net earnings? What if someone's income is on a steep upward trajectory? What should go into determining a starting point for alimony and child support? Should the court take into consideration these possibilities and not just the last year or two or five?

I think that a better method exists for answering such questions, but in the meantime, I've seen more than a few of my clients suffer unfairly due to a focus on just their recent histories rather than the overall circumstances of their cases. Just something to keep in mind for anyone considering a New Jersey divorce.

# CHAPTER 9

## *What Factors May Complicate a New Jersey Divorce?*

**At their initial consultation** with my firm, many prospective clients will tell me that their divorce should be simple, but experience has taught me that such an assessment is almost always wrong. The fact remains, however, that one of the biggest concerns clients have when contemplating divorce is how time consuming and expensive it will be.

I have been redesigning my firm's billing practices lately in an attempt to create a more uniform retainer amount. In doing so, I've thought about some of the factors that may complicate a New Jersey divorce. Here's a list of some of the factors leaving room for the possibility of others.

- one or both parties being unreasonable
- negative emotions
- one of the parties deciding not to retain an attorney
- one party retaining an attorney who takes unreasonable positions
- children particularly if custody is contested

- high-asset cases, those involving retirement accounts, stock options, or other more- sophisticated financial instruments
- one or both parties owning a business or a professional practice that needs to be evaluated
- the status of a case changed shortly before a filing for divorce
- if a forensic accountant, employability expert, or other such experts is required
- when there are domestic-violence issues or allegations
- when there are jurisdictional or venue issues
- when there are tax or bankruptcy issues or high levels of debt for one or both parties
- when one or both parties recently received a promotion or lost a job

## WHAT CAN BE DONE TO SIMPLIFY A NEW JERSEY DIVORCE?

I wrote this book to try to answer that question. As you know by now, I believe it's so necessary for those who are contemplating divorce to learn the law, accept their responsibilities under the law, and work with counselors or other professionals as necessary to ensure they have clear minds and emotions under control throughout the decision-making process.

Each party has a great deal of control over the outcome of a case; they should thus act in the best interests of their children and try to preserve family wealth even post-divorce. I want to work with such clients in those regards. My clients and I cannot completely control the other side's actions, but that I think is all the more reason to control our responses.

## CONCLUSION

I'll say it again—emotions more than anything else complicate divorces. A Marital Settlement Agreement will be more complicated if there is a business or a great deal of assets, but any divorce can be made much smoother when the parties attempt to cooperate and when necessary compromise.

Divorce can be made much smoother when the parties attempt to cooperate and **when necessary** compromise.

# CHAPTER 10

## *Does My Spouse Have to Retain an Attorney?*

**I attend** the annual New Jersey Family Law Symposium; that's where New Jersey family law practitioners meet to catch up on the latest developments in the law and to network with one another. One of the topics I discussed with a couple of practitioners I'm friends with is how it can sometimes be more difficult when the adversary is *pro se*—representing himself or herself.

Clients often ask me if their spouses will be required to retain an attorney, and the answer is no—neither party has to have a lawyer in a divorce case. People are required to have law-yers in criminal cases whether they are court appointed or not. However, a spouse who decides not to hire a lawyer has to sign a waiver to that effect; that will be mentioned in any Marital Settlement Agreement. And as I mentioned, no attorney can ethically represent both parties in a New Jersey divorce.

Some people choose to represent themselves because they don't want to spend the money or don't have it in the first place and can't find pro bono services. When they're not paying for lawyers, that might give them less incentive to reach an agreement with the other side; delaying doing so isn't costing them money. In addition, people in divorce cases who choose not to be represented are less likely to know divorce law, and that could lead them to make unreasonable demands or stall agreements because they just don't realize what would be to their best advantage.

Even lawyers will rarely represent themselves in divorce cases because they know someone else representing them would be less likely to become emotional about the process.

## CONCLUSION

Every case will have its difficulties, but there's no reason to stress if your spouse refuses to hire an attorney. It'll cost you to hire an attorney, but you'll be paying for your attorney's experience and knowledge, and that can tip the cost-benefit ratio in your favor.

## CHAPTER 11

# Helping Children through a Divorce

## An Interview with Glenn Murphy, MA, LPC

Those who divorce have to deal with their children's emotions as well as their own. To that end, I asked Glenn Murphy, MA, LPC, a well-respected New Jersey counselor, if I could interview him regarding how divorcing or separating parents can help children through a divorce. He graciously agreed, and the following is the transcript of the interview.

Please note that the following is general advice; as with legal issues, emotional or other issues are best handled by experts. For information on how to address your specific issues, contact an appropriate specialist or expert.

I thank Glenn for his contribution to this book, and I think everyone will find his answers to be thoughtful, informative, and interesting.

## INTERVIEW TRANSCRIPT

### 1. *WHAT CAN PARENTS DO TO INSULATE THEIR CHILDREN FROM THE BAD EFFECTS OF A DIVORCE OR SEPARATION?*

Given the extensive short and long-term impact of divorce on everyone, couples would ideally commit to working hard on healing their marriages and would see divorce or separation as a last resort.

Weekend marriage rebuilding intensives like those offered at Retrouvaille and MarriageMinistry.org can help couples begin the restoration process even after an affair. Marital therapy with a professional counselor or psychologist would also be a highly recommended aspect of the healing and recovery plan that hopefully would help protect children from the pain and scars of divorce.

### 2. *HOW DOES DIVORCE AFFECT CHILDREN AT AGES FIVE, TEN, FIFTEEN, AND THEN ON INTO THEIR COLLEGE YEARS AND ADULTHOOD?*

Very young children generally lack the ability to process what is happening or why it is happening. They might blame themselves for the divorce or believe it's their responsibility to try to get their parents back together. They'll often become clingy or show other signs of distress such as regressing behaviorally.

By age ten, children are more able to understand what is happening yet will likely experience intense grief and sadness over not living with both parents. They will likely express strong feelings of disapproval and anger at what is happening to them and may take sides deciding who is the "good" parent and who is the "bad" parent. Boys will tend to go inside themselves and shut down while girls will tend to go outside themselves and verbally express their emotions. Children at that age may also become more manipulative and try to use their parents' guilt to get whatever they want.

Among adolescents, you might anticipate boys expressing themselves more aggressively and acting more defiantly toward parental authority. They may also seek escapes such as video games and pot as a way to distract and numb themselves from the pain they feel.

Girls may become more anxious and begin acting out sexually seeking comfort or escape in relationships with guys. Parents might also anticipate their teenagers blaming them for "ruining my life."

College-age children of divorce tend to be more skeptical of marriage, love, and commitment. They may have difficulty making decisions or make rash decisions, and they may view marriage as a trap they want to avoid. They may be more interested in no-strings attached hookups as a means of protecting themselves emotionally.

Depending on whom they see as the good or bad parent, they may take on the role of mom's protector or dad's defender. Over time, they will likely begin letting go of these roles and adapt to the new reality of their two families especially if mom and dad have resolved their hostilities peacefully. Conversely, they may a distance themselves from one or both parents especially if the pain from their family of origin remains unresolved in ongoing parent wars.

### 3. HOW CAN PARENTS PREPARE THEIR CHILDREN FOR A PENDING DIVORCE?

Ideally, parents should talk together with their children about their intention to divorce in advance so the children would have some time to begin to process it, ask questions, and know what will be happening. That conversation would include information about where they will be living and any other changes that will be impacting their lives.

If both parents will be actively involving in parenting, that should be mentioned to provide appropriate reassurance and stabilization. Additionally, children should be assured of their parents' ongoing commitment to and love for them. Children need to know they won't get lost, forgotten, or neglected in the midst of the marriage crisis. I cannot stress this point enough as children are likely to wonder, *If your love for each other ended, how do I know it won't also end for me when we're no longer living together every day or when one or both of you remarry?*

### 4. WHAT SHOULD PARENT TELL THEIR CHILDREN AFTER A DECISION HAS BEEN MADE TO SEPARATE OR DIVORCE? SHOULD BOTH PARENTS BE PRESENT TO BREAK SUCH NEWS?

Ideally, parents would avoid pointing fingers and blaming their partners. Wise parents would choose instead to use more-neutral language even if they do internally blame their spouses for an impending divorce. Children are too easily put in the middle, a place they don't belong. *We* should be the operative word, not *your father* or *your mother.* The children should be told, "We have reached the point where we will no longer remain married and living together." If possible, both parents should be present for this conversation, and they should prepare ahead of time with each other for that conversation.

(Other key elements of that conversation are outlined in question 3.)

### 5. WHAT ARE SOME WARNING SIGNS THAT MARITAL OR DIVORCE ISSUES ARE NEGATIVELY AFFECTING CHILDREN?

It should be anticipated that all divorces will negatively affect children in some fashion. So rather than hoping to avoid any negative impact, it might be better for parents to watch for indications that the negative affect is falling outside the normal range. For example, being angry and expressing one's anger over the divorce is normal, but expressing that anger by punching holes in bedroom walls is outside that range.

Likewise, having children exhibit increased anxiety might be expected, but not being able to sleep at night or engaging in self-harming behavior designed to relieve that anxiety such as cutting is a cry for help. Parents should also be on the alert for signals such as dramatic weight gain or weight loss, school grades declining, loss of interests in previously enjoyed activities, withdrawing from close friends—any signs that suggests children are not coping or adapting but rather are in a state of declining health, functionality or well-being.

### 6. AT WHAT POINT SHOULD A PARENT CONSIDER COUNSELING FOR A CHILD TO HELP THE CHILD DEAL WITH THE PARENTS' DIVORCE OR SEPARATION?

As stated in the previous answer, when a parent observes that the child's coping skills and internal resources are not sufficient to meet the challenges brought on by divorce, that's the time to seek counseling. If you've given them some time to grieve the loss and sought to personally help them adapt to their new normal but they only continue to destabilize and decompensate, seek professional help.

### 7. WHEN ISSUES OF DOMESTIC VIOLENCE ARE INVOLVED, HOW DOES THAT CHANGE YOUR APPROACH TO CHILDREN'S THERAPY?

Domestic violence can change the approach to therapy; it may necessitate the therapist's helping the children to detach from the abusive parent until that parent gets help and becomes a safer, nonviolent person. This is obviously a very different approach than that of the therapist helping the child to maintain a strong bond with both parents throughout the divorce process as would be more typical in a case where domestic violence is not present.

### 8. ASSUMING NO COURT ORDERS OR LAWS ARE IN PLACE ADDRESSING THIS ISSUE, HOW MUCH INFORMATION SHOULD YOUNGER CHILDREN BE TOLD ABOUT THEIR PARENTS' DIVORCE?

There is no simple or easy way to explain divorce to a young child, but it's normally best to provide truthful but not specific details. For example, details such as "Your daddy has been paying woman to have sex with him" is way too much information for young children; they don't have the capacity to understand the complexities that are typically involved in divorce, nor are they able to process some of the more painful and explicit details about parental mistakes, but they can understand concepts like happiness and unhappiness and the parents' desire to stop fighting each other.

### 9. WHAT SHOULD BOTH PARENTS DO TO WORK TOGETHER TO MINIMIZE THE CHANCES THAT THEIR DIVORCE OR SEPARATION WILL NEGATIVELY IMPACT THEIR CHILDREN? WHAT'S THE BEST PARENTING ARRANGEMENT TO STIMULATE CHILDREN'S CONTINUED DEVELOPMENT?

Parents should discuss and agree to follow ground rules for the sake of the children's well-being. Examples of possible ground rules are these.

- We will not talk badly about each other to our children or in front of our children.
- We will not use our children to send messages to each other or interrogate them after visiting with each other.
- We will not undermine each other's house rules or daily decisions.
- We will discuss and mutually work out between ourselves the larger decisions that will obligate or involve us.
- We will seek opportunities to point out to our children the good qualities of each other and model respect for them.

The best parenting arrangement would include parents who are equally committed to making parenting a priority, who share custody, and who live close to each other to minimize disruption and chaos in their children's routines and schedules. Children of divorced families do best when parenting schedules and times are regular, predictable, and occur without drama or conflict when they're being picked up or dropped off.

## 10. WHAT ARE SOME RESOURCES FOR PARENTS TO USE IN HELPING THEIR CHILDREN DURING A SEPARATION AND DIVORCE?

Groups for children of divorce can be helpful for children navigating the divorce process. Children often benefit from having a safe place where they can talk with a safe adult facilitator and with other children going through the same experience. They need to be able to freely express their feelings and grieve their losses without fear that they're hurting mom or dad by what they say.

Check with your children's schools' guidance counselors, mental health centers, or church or other religious organization to see if they run such a group. There are also many helpful books written for every age group from preschool through adolescence to help children cope with the aftermath and pain of divorce.

Glenn Murphy is a longtime New Jersey Licensed Professional Counselor (LPC). He maintains a full-time psychotherapy and counseling practice in Basking Ridge, New Jersey, where he works with adolescents, adults, individuals, and couples. For more information about his services, please visit his website: GlennMurphyCounseling.com.

# CHAPTER 12

# Mediation— Coaching and Counseling

As I note throughout this book, emotions play an important part in divorces. If emotions can be effectively harnessed, divorces can be much more amicable and more likely to lead to a positive result for those involved.

I am very familiar with how emotions can affect a divorce for good and for ill, but I am a divorce lawyer with no formal training as a counselor. For that reason, I often advise my clients to obtain independent counseling, life coaching, or other forms of stress relief during their divorces, and I frequently refer my clients to professionals trained in addressing such issues.

One such person is my friend Debra Pirozzoli, who has contributed the following chapter on the issue of life coaching and how to best address emotions in divorce situations. This guest chapter also addresses how your actions may affect your children not just during a divorce but also throughout their lives.

Mediation is a process of achieving resolution for a common good. Its chief advantage is that it can reduce financial and emotional burdens.

When anger and sadness are the dominant emotions in a marriage, the spouses' vision for the future becomes distorted. However, when professional life-coaching and counseling become part of the process, families are able to reconstruct their family dynamic without destroying the entire structure. But what does that mean?

A family is a flexible system. When people no longer choose to live in the once-familiar structure, a new one may be developed. So many people who choose to divorce make decisions based on impulses, which may be self-destructive to the family and its members. These impulse behaviors include revenge, which may grow like a cancer. Rather, the parties should develop a dynamic that is constructive, one that produces less loss and anxiety. This is also a structure that protects the emotional welfare of the children involved in the change.

One of the most important aspects of change is the ability to look beyond the hurt and pain to ascertain what is best for the children. Change in the midst of a storm does not have to produce victims. Each parent can choose a strategy that will be different but still produce unity even in the most trying circumstances.

This process includes being aware of what I call emotional hemophilia. Otherwise, the result can be an increase in impulsive behavior, confusion, and anger. I consider it wise for the parents to work with the same mediator-coach so they can be counseled for success. This coach will be an objective advisor at a time when sorting out the details of how to reconstruct the family system can seem overwhelming. When this is accomplished, the results produce minimal suffering for the family system. Children ought to be allowed to be simply children, not kids caught in the middle. Once children take on the negative aspects of divorce, it is difficult for everyone to correct their course.

Just imagine how children suffer when things they cherish break or are lost; it's like the end of the world to them. Imagine what goes through the minds of children who have to live in the midst of chaos in the most important dynamic in their lives. One day, life seems safe, and the next, it seems insecure.

The good news is that when parents learn new skills, it's as if they have learned a new language. This new dynamic produces a rearranged system that can benefit all the members of a family. Thus, all who are involved will be able to function at a heightened level and develop a new norm that will give them hope for a changed family dynamic with the fewest destructive behaviors. The notion is to recreate a new system, not to break the old one into pieces.

## SPLITTING THE FAMILY

At first glance, the words *splitting the family* can heighten emotions, but when we split something, it takes on a whole new context. No matter how hurt parents can be when their lives change, their children's emotional well-being will be governed by how they view this change, and that's governed largely by how the parents choose to share. That sounds elementary, doesn't it? Yes, this is basic, relational skill building as one learns to change without getting into a tug-of-war.

When children are caught in the middle of divorce, it is best to talk with them in a way that change does not equal "bad." Change can in fact be good. Moving to a new house can take some getting used to, but it doesn't have to be a bad experience. We can remind children of a time, for instance, that they switched schools; they may have had concerns about the change, but it ultimately ended up being positive.

The outcome depends on the atmosphere parents created. It is wise to train ourselves and our children to accept change. Based on the parents' behavior, they may destroy the atmosphere and create a storm that interrupts their ability to create a new vision, or they may create the possibility for a *Happily Even After*.

## STORMY RELATIONSHIPS

In a storm, the atmosphere changes. Maturity or lack of it becomes evident as those caught up in the chaos of a divorce or fractured relationship take on new roles. Many times, parents proclaim that their children are fine, but being naive about children's emotional states often produces teens and young adults who become addicted to a variety of escapes.

A child's emotional well-being will be governed by how they view this change, and that's governed largely by how the parents choose to share.

Our schools are filled with children from divorced families, and many parents are aware of the staggering numbers but consider that a sort of new norm. However, children are increasingly using drugs and alcohol, being promiscuous, and committing suicide at younger and younger ages. This has become an epidemic, and children of divorced or fractured families are at an increased risk of such negative outcomes if their parents inappropriately put their children in the middle of a divorce or a contentious relationship. It is thus wise to think about how much our society has changed, be prepared to go into the reconstructed family system, and do some prevention instead of damage control. Doing that requires new skills.

We work with families and teach skills for developing new norms and new roles, and the outcomes have produced healthier and more-productive children who as a result of less chaos are able to withstand their storms. Families that divide in unity but develop a new norm without breaking trust with children and work on developing safety experience fewer and less-severe emotional casualties.

We are excited to be a positive part of our clients' experience. Below is our contact information should you believe such coaching/counseling is appropriate for your situation. Please ask for more information, and don't hesitate to make an appointment to mediate with a counseling coach to create a new family structure or system with the least amount of pain and emotional casualty for all involved.

*Chapter contributed by:*

**Debra A. Pirozzoli,** MS, CMPC, LCPC, CTC
Marriage, Family & Individual Counseling Center
Executive Life Coaching
908-642-7238

# CHAPTER 13

# The Nuts and Bolts of the New Jersey Divorce Procedure

**When you're going through a divorce** in New Jersey, you'll often feel confused about what the next steps will be. You'll receive court notices for mandatory parenting classes and wonder if the court is judging your parenting skills. You'll receive other court notices with odd acronyms such as ESP and ISC and wonder what they mean. By familiarizing yourself with the basic procedures below, you'll have a roadmap for the flow of a New Jersey divorce.

## BASIC OUTLINE OF A NEW JERSEY DIVORCE

A contested New Jersey divorce can take months or even years to settle. A divorce may also take years to be finalized if the case goes to trial. Appropriate aggressive techniques to expedite favorable settlement negotiations will often be employed on your behalf to limit cost and maximize results.

One major point to be aware of is that a divorce can essentially end at any time once both parties agree to the divorce terms in a document generally called the Marital Settlement

Agreement (MSA). A divorce is finalized about a month after both parties sign off on it. Some divorces settle amicably before either party files, other cases resolve with the help of mediators, others enter arbitration, and others go all the way to trial. But regardless of the track taken, the case will resolve only after both parties agree in writing to the MSA or if not, the court hears a trial and makes its determination about the divorce terms.

The outline below is by no means exhaustive; there are several alternative dispute-resolution processes available in New Jersey divorce matters including mediation or collaborative law as mentioned in chapter 8. Such methods may be the least expensive and most efficient ways of working toward a divorce, but in certain cases, clients will require aggressive representation to protect their interests.

The list below assumes that mediation or other alternative dispute-resolution processes are not something you wish to pursue or perhaps cannot pursue because of domestic violence or other issues that may render mediation impractical or impossible. In some cases, alternative methods might not give you the results you want.

1. Determining whether a divorce is the right decision for you
2. Choosing an attorney or deciding to represent yourself
3. Pleadings and Case Information Statements
4. Case Management Conferences
5. Beginning negotiations
6. Discovery
7. Continuing negotiations/drafting a Marital Settlement Agreement (MSA)

8. Early Settlement Panel (ESP)
9. Court-ordered economic mediation
10. All-day Intensive Settlement Conference (ISC)
11. Going to court and have a judge rule on contested matters

I know what you're probably thinking—*I don't know what half of it means! What does discovery involve? What is an Early Settlement Panel?* Don't worry. I explain each step in the next chapter. But first, let's review what constitutes the different acceptable grounds for divorce in New Jersey.

## GROUNDS FOR DIVORCE IN NEW JERSEY

There are various grounds for divorce in New Jersey, which long ago moved away from more fault-based counts as a requirement. As you'll see below, most people today file under irreconcilable differences unless there is a distinct tactical advantage to utilizing one of the fault-based counts.

### 1. IRRECONCILABLE DIFFERENCES

This is the most common grounds for divorce in New Jersey despite the fact that it was only recently recognized by the state. Irreconcilable differences is essentially an expedited form of no-fault divorce. The major statutory requirement is that what are called irreconcilable differences have occurred that caused the breakdown of the marriage, that there is no prospect of reconciliation, and that these irreconcilable differences have been ongoing for at least six months.

Only one party needs to seek a divorce as in New Jersey there is no requirement that both parties agree to divorce. Your spouse cannot deny your filing a divorce complaint in New Jersey, but he or she could tie up the divorce process by forcing a trial.

Irreconcilable differences is essentially an expedited form of no-fault divorce.

## 2. NO FAULT

New Jersey law says that a couple who live apart for at least eighteen consecutive months with no reasonable prospect for reconciliation can divorce on that basis. These requirements make no-fault divorce rare in New Jersey, so most divorcing couples take the irreconcilable-differences route.

## 3. EXTREME MENTAL OR PHYSICAL CRUELTY

The rest of the grounds for divorce are more fault-based. A claim of extreme mental or physical cruelty requires proof of "any physical or mental cruelty which endangers the safety or health of the plaintiff or makes it improper or unreasonable to expect the Plaintiff to continue to cohabit with the Defendant."

## 4. ADULTERY

Clients often ask about using adultery as grounds for divorce; the problem is establishing adultery through circumstantial or other evidence. Moreover, the suspected partner in the alleged infidelity must then be named in the complaint and served as a correspondent to the divorce.

Using adultery as grounds for divorce in New Jersey is often so time consuming and expensive that it's not worth the effort.

And the benefits of an adultery claim are in most cases minimal if they exist at all. The court rules do not "punish" an adulterer in terms of alimony or equitable distribution. At best, it may show a lack of fitness as a parent in certain cases.

And because New Jersey is a no-fault state, even if someone is more to blame for the breakdown of the marriage, he or she will not generally be punished in any way in the divorce.

## 5. OTHER GROUNDS

Other New Jersey grounds for divorce are available, but they are exceedingly rare. They include

- desertion
- deviant sexual behavior
- imprisonment
- institutionalization
- habitual drunkenness or drug habituation

In certain cases, a Complaint for Divorce in New Jersey could include more than one or all the above counts.

Now that you're familiar with the different grounds for divorce in New Jersey, let's familiarize ourselves with the uncontested-divorce process.

## UNCONTESTED DIVORCES

Most people don't want to be involved in long, expensive, and drawn-out litigation if there's an amicable path forward. To that end, an uncontested divorce may make more sense for the clients than protracted divorce litigation.

Of course, negotiating a settlement will not always be easy, but the goal of both parties should generally be to be open to favorable settlement terms. At the same time, cases settle favorably based on leverage, and thus even when the goal is to quickly settle a case, it may be appropriate to consider aggressive discovery techniques, motion practices, and other actions to create additional leverage to reach a favorable settlement.

## NEW JERSEY UNCONTESTED-DIVORCE HEARINGS

A New Jersey uncontested-divorce hearing will be scheduled when the parties reach a settlement and advise the court of that and their readiness to finalize their divorce. An uncontested-divorce hearing is perhaps somewhat ironically one of the least complex parts of the entire divorce process.

The plaintiff and his or her attorney (assuming the plaintiff has counsel) will attend the uncontested hearing. The defendant and his or her counsel will often choose to attend as well though that's not required provided the defendant hasn't filed a counterclaim.

The parties will then be asked certain questions by their counsel to establish a "cause of action" and show that the settlement agreement is valid and was willingly entered into. The cause of action is the grounds for the divorce such as irreconcilable differences or extreme cruelty. Because New Jersey is a no-fault divorce state, divorces proceed as long as one of the parties want it to go on.

The judge may follow up with a few additional questions though he or she will not make a determination as to whether the agreement is fair and equitable.

## MEDIATION

One particularly effective method for working toward an uncontested divorce is attending mediation. Both parties will likely retain their own counsel to assist them and will then choose a mutually acceptable mediator (generally splitting the cost). The parties (generally with assistance from their attorneys) will then attempt to reach an understanding—a Memorandum of Understanding, an MOU. After that, one of the attorneys will draft a settlement agreement.

Mediation is generally an expedited and less-expensive method of finalizing a divorce, but it isn't favored in cases involving a history of domestic violence or when one party will not be able to hold his or her own during the mediation process either with or without a lawyer.

## AFTER THE UNCONTESTED-DIVORCE HEARING

After that, the parties will be given gold-sealed copies of their Judgment of Divorce. It is important to keep this copy and the Marital Settlement Agreement, the MSA, which is sometimes referred to as the Property Settlement Agreement (PSA), in a safe place should some unresolved issues or other post-divorce loose ends or business to be taken care of. Your attorney should offer guidance regarding these issues. One thing to consider is immediately changing your will and life insurance policies so your ex won't remain as a beneficiary.

The uncontested-divorce hearing is a day of closure, most likely a bittersweet day for both parties. It's an end and a beginning.

Your attorney should notify you of what to expect the day of the hearing, review the uncontested-divorce questions with you in advance, and later advise you of how to tie up post-divorce loose ends and determine whether you wish for continued representation relating to such issues as dividing marital assets or implementing other clauses in the agreement.

But if litigation becomes inevitable, you will begin taking steps toward a contested divorce, which I've outlined below. But first, let's review some of the major divorce issues.

## CHAPTER 14

# *The 11-Step Divorce Litigation Process*

## STEP 1: IS DIVORCE REALLY THE ANSWER?

As I mentioned earlier, some prospective clients walk into my office and are absolutely sure their marriages are over and they're ready to file for divorce. Others aren't sure if they're ready for divorce; they're just exploring their options if they choose to go that route. What they really want is an overview of their rights and obligations and what they should expect if they choose to file for divorce.

Some clients don't want to divorce but their spouses do; that usually puts them in an emotional bind. Divorce is tough on everyone, but it can be tougher on someone who doesn't want to get divorced. I recommend to such people that they seek counseling. I provide them—and I'll provide you—with referrals to counselors and therapists.

Some rocky marriages are indeed salvageable. I'm no psychologist or a marriage therapist, so I can never say whether a client's marriage is or isn't worth attempting to save; only the client can answer that really personal decision. But I often do recommend that parties (except in extreme cases such as those involving abuse) try marriage counseling before initiating a divorce. If nothing else, this process may assist the parties understand each other and the reasons divorce may be necessary.

Before you start a divorce proceeding, take whatever time you need to be sure that the chances of saving your marriage are slim to none. Once you've settled that question, you can then begin with the divorce process full-speed ahead and with a clear conscience about your decisions and objectives and choose an attorney.

## STEP 2: CHOOSING AN ATTORNEY

As I mentioned, some people decide to represent themselves in a divorce, but many seek the help of an attorney who specializes in divorce to help them protect their rights.

When you're interviewing, as I call it, attorneys, make sure they're licensed to practice in New Jersey and that their practices emphasize family law. Ask about costs as there will be a wide range of hourly rates and retainer amounts. You can find attorneys through referrals, through local bar associations, and on the internet.

Once these basic considerations have been met, your next step is to determine the right attorney for you. Personality plays a key role in divorce cases, and good rapport between client and attorney can be crucial to maximizing the gains and limiting the risks.

The attorney-client relationship will likely last months or even years from the first consultation until the divorce is finalized, so personality will be more important than you might think. I've handled dozens of divorces for clients, and though the law has remained largely the same, each case was defined not just by specific facts but by the personalities of the parties and their attorneys.

Competence and experience are always important when choosing any professional. Most people today prefer attorneys who work predominantly in divorce cases or who limit their practice to only a few key areas of law.

Effective representation includes teaching and advising you about the law and divorce procedure, coordinating with you to design and implement an effective litigation strategy, and outlining appropriate objectives that maximize your leverage and limit your exposure. A good attorney should be honest about what objectives are likely achievable and discuss both best-case and worst-case scenarios. After an initial consultation, attorney and client should understand their expectations of each other for the case, their responsibilities and rights, and whether they want to work together.

## STEP 3: PLEADINGS AND THE CASE INFORMATION STATEMENT

Although this has not always been the case, New Jersey divorce pleadings today are fairly straightforward. The point of divorce pleadings isn't to prove your whole case but rather to lay out all the relevant causes of action. Except with claims of marital tort or extreme cruelty or the like, pleadings will be general in nature compared to most other types of litigation. New Jersey divorce pleadings are not required to be technical; all that's required is that basic facts be set forth that demonstrate the underlying claims. Pleadings must also indicate the type(s) of relief requested. Under the relevant court rules, alternative forms of relief may be requested in the pleadings.

Perhaps the most important concept to remember regarding pleadings is this—New Jersey courts understand that you're at the very beginning of the litigation process. Therefore, the rules are generally lenient provided that a factual basis for the relief requested is provided. But it's also important to remember to plead every cause of action in the underlying claim. If you don't, you could be barred from bringing up pleadings later. All pleadings and particularly complaints are important and should be taken seriously.

## RES JUDICATA AND THE ENTIRE CONTROVERSY DOCTRINE

Res judicata means this: "You must now bring every cause of action that stems from the underlying claim with your present pleadings, or you may be barred from retrying or seeking relief for the same issues at a later court appearance." It's somewhat similar to the concept that people cannot be put in double jeopardy—tried for the same crime twice. It means that you cannot later add on a complaint of extreme mental cruelty, for instance, after claiming irreconcilable differences in your original filing.

### THREE MAJOR TYPES OF PLEADINGS IN A NEW JERSEY DIVORCE

- complaint (and summons)
- answer/counterclaim
- answer to the answer/counterclaim

There are filing fees required by the court in connection with the filing of a complaint or an answer to a complaint, and there are deadlines for filing them. Some manner of answer or appearance is required within thirty-five days of the date the defendant receives a summons or complaint. Otherwise, the court may start the default-judgment process against the defendant.

The pleadings also set forth the cause or causes of action. Some of the more popular divorce causes of action include irreconcilable differences, adultery, and extreme cruelty among others with irreconcilable differences being utilized a vast majority of the time as New Jersey is a no-fault state.

New Jersey divorce pleadings formally initiate the divorce litigation process. It is important that all the court rules are followed so that the case can begin properly.

## CASE INFORMATION STATEMENT (CIS)

The Case Information Statement is often referred to as the most important financial document in New Jersey family law matters. In it, each party lists assets, liabilities, personal information, and living expenses. If the case ever comes back in post-judgment matters, it will be (along with the agreement) the most important document for purposes of proving changed circumstances.

By court rule, a CIS must be filed within twenty days after filing an answer/counterclaim. After you retain our firm, we will provide you with specific instructions on this and walk you through the CIS process.

Both parties are required to fill out CISs to let the other side know about finances and other documentation so both parties will be aware of where they stand.

## STEP 4: CASE MANAGEMENT CONFERENCES (CMCS)

Shortly after the pleadings have been finalized, the case will likely be assigned its first Case Management Conference (CMC). The major purpose of a CMC is to create deadlines for discovery and other court processes. In most counties, if the parties can agree to a case management order, they will not be required to attend the first CMC.

Around the same time, if you have children, you may receive a court notice for a mandatory parenting class. Don't take this personally as it truly is mandatory for all contested matters involving children. Your spouse will also have to attend a separate class. The class has absolutely no bearing on your case provided that you don't miss it. You can reschedule it, but your attorney will have to send a letter requesting that.

The class is simply a program the court created to give divorcing parents the resources they need to handle their future parenting responsibilities and to encourage both parties to do their best to resolve their matters amicably and in their children's best interests.

## STEP 5: BEGINNING NEGOTIATIONS

It's best to shine some light on contested issues that must be resolved. Even in the most complex or most highly contested divorces, there are often many issues the parties agree on. The basic issues that need to be resolved in the average New Jersey divorce include the following:

- equitable distribution of marital property including retirement accounts, debts, businesses, and the marital home or other real property

- alimony
- child support
- custody
- educational costs for children
- insurance issues
- counsel fees
- parenting time

## STEP 6: DISCOVERY

Discovery is the process of seeking and providing information. It may require providing years of bank statements, income tax returns, credit card statements, retirement account information, and much more. Though it can be easy, it can become very time consuming and expensive if, say, it requires outside experts to evaluate the value of a business or professional practice, to determine the employability of a spouse who might not be working at the time, and so on. It's a subject that can get so involved that it's largely beyond what I'm trying to do in this book. That said, discovery is quite important particularly if you suspect the other party is hiding assets or engaging in other suspicious behavior.

Some of the basic discovery methods include interrogatories, admissions, requests for production of documents, authorizations, subpoenas, and in some instances getting the depositions of the other party. It can be a very effective way of getting admissions from the opposing party and thus gaining leverage.

## STEP 7: CONTINUING NEGOTIATIONS AND THE MARITAL SETTLEMENT AGREEMENT

Sometimes, the divorce process can become so bogged down in minutiae and emotional baggage that the final destination—almost always a formal divorce—becomes obscured. Divorce attorneys understand that it's much more than that. If a divorce is properly resolved, it should give the parties a sense of closure. There will always be a few loose ends, but an effective Divorce Agreement must attempt to crystallize the parties' intent and provide a roadmap for how to handle future issues. This is the role of New Jersey Marital Settlement Agreements (MSA), which are also called Divorce Agreements or Property Settlement Agreements.

For better or worse, most parties to a divorce will continue to maintain some sort of relationship with each other due to their children, friends, and other issues. A divorce is the ultimate goal, but after that, the MSA will in many ways become the law of the divorce moving forward—where the children will spend their holidays and summers, how often they'll get to see both parents, and so on. It provides a structure for the former family's lives from that point on.

An MSA will generally incorporate language addressing issues that are expected to come up after a divorce. One might read, "Husband shall have parenting time with the children each Thanksgiving from 8:00 a.m., until 3:00 p.m.., and the Wife shall have parenting time with the children each Thanksgiving after 3:00 p.m." Another might read, "Wife shall have Thanksgiving parenting time in odd years and the Husband in even years."

An MSA that doesn't lay out the rules for such matters might necessitate further court intervention. I've had a few clients tell me that this level of detail is not necessary because the parties will work it out between themselves. That might be the case for some parties, but it doesn't leave a fallback position should otherwise amicable relationships sour post-divorce. Such terms may be relaxed between the parties just as the rules of a board game can be relaxed by mutual agreement, but if that agreement isn't there, the MSA will prevail.

An MSA encapsulates the disposition of issues in a divorce. It should address the items described above and include but not be limited to matters of child support, equitable distribution of assets, alimony or a waiver of alimony, and much more.

The laws about alimony and equitable distribution of assets can be extremely complex. Employability issues, salary, whether someone is a W-2 wage earner or a business owner or both, whether assets are marital or exempt as gifted, inherited, or pre-marital, and many other complex issues involving potential tax ramifications, pension distributions, stock options, and the like may all be included in an MSA. It is important that all relevant issues be agreed within reason prior to entry of the divorce and executed in a formal written agreement.

In sum, no agreement can include a contingency for every possible issue that might come up, but it's important to cover every conceivable important issue as part of the divorce resolution.

New Jersey MSAs are probably the most important document overall in the divorce process. They along with the Case Information Statement will be used as evidence should the need for future court appearances be required, for example, to modify child support.

It's important that the MSA is very detailed, that your attorney has crafted the terms to incorporate the full agreement, and that it's fair. It's not unusual for MSAs to be modified ten or more times prior to the parties signing it even in uncontested divorces, but it's far better to go through that process before the divorce is finalized than to have to go back to court to address something the agreement didn't cover.

## STEP 8: EARLY SETTLEMENT PANEL

If you pursue New Jersey divorce litigation far enough, you'll be required to attend an Early Settlement Panel (ESP). Essentially, in New Jersey, an ESP is a required, court-ordered form of non-binding arbitration. On the day of an ESP, both parties (and their attorneys if they have them) attend court for a meeting with early settlement panelists.

The panelists will meet with the attorneys and later with the parties. Some of the procedures vary from county to county in New Jersey, but most counties require some form of legal memorandum or legal documentation from each of the parties prior to the day of the ESP.

The members of an ESP are usually two experienced family law attorneys in the specific county who volunteer their time. They'll generally ask the attorneys to review the major outstanding issues. What they'll try to do is endorse a settlement or see if they can help the parties jump over their hurdles. This is one of many ways the court system helps control its docket and reduce the number of divorces it has to deal with.

Without the clients present, the lawyers will lay out their arguments. After that, the parties will generally be brought in, and the panelists will give their opinions on how the judge would decide the outstanding issues. The idea is that the party with an unreasonable position or demand will realize he or she likely won't prevail in court, become willing to drop their un-supportable positions, and agree to a fair settlement. But since what the panelists will recommend isn't binding, they can't force either party to budge.

ESPs are important even if their recommendations aren't binding in that they can affect the tenor of future negotiations, and their efforts might convince both sides to settle.

## STEP 9: COURT-ORDERED ECONOMIC MEDIATION

If you didn't settle the case at the ESP level or shortly thereafter, most counties will require you to attend mandatory economic mediation. The court will provide a list of mediators—generally attorneys with mediation experience. The parties and their law-yers will meet with a mediator to attempt to resolve financial issues between the parties.

Under New Jersey court rules, the mediator's first two hours are volunteered and thus not billed. After that, the parties can continue mediation and be billed at the mediator's regular rate. This is another way New Jersey tries to reduce case backlogs and not eat up courts' and judges' time.

## STEP 10: INTENSIVE SETTLEMENT CONFERENCE

The Intensive Settlement Conference (ISC) is the last step, the last stop, before a trial. In an ISC, the parties and their attorneys are required to come to court and stay there all day until they hash out their differences or the court closes for the day. If they can't reach an agreement, the assumption is that a trial will take place. But even then, the parties could settle before and even during a trial.

## STEP 11: THE TRIAL

A New Jersey divorce trial is another topic too big and complex to address in one book, but I offer here some information about the process. For one, a trial likely won't be continuous. You might be called in on, say, March 3 for half a day, come back on March 18 for a full day, and pick it up again sometime in May. After that, it may take months for a judge to write his or her opinion. In short, it's generally a slow and costly process. That's why the vast majority of New Jersey divorces settle prior to trial.

It's important to prepare yourself emotionally for a trial even though the majority of cases settle prior to trial. That will allows you to gain leverage and negotiate from a position of strength. If you prepare yourself well for a trial, ironically, you'll often be better able to settle the case without a trial.

Every case is fact sensitive, so you should review all the available grounds for divorce with your attorney to ensure you select the proper grounds for your case.

## CONCLUSION

I hope you've found this chapter helpful and that you now possess a greater understanding of the New Jersey divorce process itself. If you've already retained my services, I look forward to working with you or continuing to work with you. If you're considering my services and would like to schedule an initial consultation, please contact me at 908-685-0900.

# CHAPTER 15

# An Overview of Relevant New Jersey Divorce Law

## CHILD SUPPORT LAW IN NEW JERSEY

Child support in New Jersey is an obligation that runs from parent to child rather than from parent to parent. When viewed through this prism, child-support law in New Jersey becomes more easily understood.

## DETERMINING CHILD SUPPORT IN NEW JERSEY

In most instances, the amount of child support will be determined by New Jersey's Child Support Guidelines that involve some complicated formulas based on:

- both parties' income from all sources (earned and unearned including alimony),
- the amount of overnight parenting time exercised by each parent,
- the children's ages,
- health-care and child-care costs, and
- support paid for children from another relationship.

As the New Jersey Child Support Guidelines are formulas, most disputes involve the methodology or actual data input. For instance, a party may argue that a spouse earns a substantial but unreported sum of money from, say, tips, and that would affect that spouse's actual income and thus the amount he or she could be expected to pay for child support.

Parents who are not the residential parent—the one who doesn't have the children for most of the time—believe they have to pay or are paying for all their children's support. In most instances, however, that's not so. Parents who are the primary residential parents may or may not have a probation account, an account to which the ex pays alimony and is then sent to the one who is supposed to receive it, but they pay for all the children's expenses not covered by the child-support payments; they cannot expect the nonresidential parents' child support to cover all their children's expenses. Except in very rare instances, neither party has the obligation to pay for all of their children's support; it's a shared obligation.

## DEVIATION FROM THE CHILD-SUPPORT GUIDELINES

In some cases, the child-support guidelines will not be used or will deviate from the agreed-upon amount. That's the case when an adult child resides away from home during college, or when the net income of both parties from all sources exceeds $187,200. In that instance, a deviation from the New Jersey Child Support Guidelines may be necessary.[1]

---

1    http://www.mynjdivorcelawyer.com/tag/new-jersey-divorce-process/#_ftn1.

## MODIFICATION OF CHILD SUPPORT IN NEW JERSEY

When a child-support account is established through Family Support Services/Probation, there will often be periodic increases in support (cost of living adjustments). Likewise, the parties may agree to revisit child support at certain set intervals such as every three years. Child support may also be modified, however, at any time if there's a significant change in circumstances. Some common examples of what may be considered a change in circumstances include these.

- modification of custody or parenting time
- changes (positive or negative) in the incomes of the parties
- job loss, serious illness, disability
- emancipation of one or more children
- termination of child support in New Jersey

Until recently, New Jersey did not assume the emancipation of a child or the termination of child support upon a child's eighteenth birthday. In fact, appellate cases even stated that a child could even be "unemancipated." However, recent legislation presumes emancipation and termination of child support once a child reaches nineteen. A parent receiving child support for someone who is nineteen or older can ask the court that the child support continue if the child is disabled, not out of high school, going to college, or other compelling reasons. The new legislation also says that emancipation must occur no later than when a child reaches age twenty-three.

In New Jersey, children are considered emancipated if they have moved beyond the "sphere and influence" of their parents, but it's rare for the court to say that a college student has moved beyond that sphere. In New Jersey, both parents are generally required to contribute to their children's college costs and at times up to and including paying toward professional or graduate degrees.

## CUSTODY LAW IN NEW JERSEY

Custody disputes can be both expensive and emotionally draining. In 1992, the appellate division court even hinted at the judiciary feeling somewhat uncomfortable with deciding custody disputes.

Specifically, in *Tahan v. Duquette*,[2] the court wrote the following opinion, which is regularly cited in other cases.

> We urge the parties to understand that courts in any jurisdiction are poor places to resolve such fundamental relational problems as child custody. Rules of law and procedural strictures are no substitute for personal choices in so intensely personal an issue. Parents who have divorced are frequently unable to communicate constructively on issues of importance; so they look to the legal system to resolve their problems. But no stranger in a judicial robe, however able and well-motivated he or she may be, is equipped to make a decision as valid as the parents working together might make.

There are few if any elements of a divorce that are more important than protecting the best interests of the parties' children.

---

2    259 N.J. Super 328, 336 (App. Div. 1992).

Likewise, there are few issues that will become as contentious as a custody dispute.

## NEW JERSEY CHILD CUSTODY: BEST INTERESTS OF THE CHILDREN STANDARD

The analysis of most child-custody disputes in New Jersey starts and ends with a simple but hard to define standard—the best interests of the child. These may include the following and more.

- Where will the child receive the best education?
- Where will the child be safest?
- Which party can provide "better" living conditions?
- Which party is more nurturing?
- Where will the child have the best chance to excel?

But no stranger in a judicial robe, however able and well-motivated he or she may be, is equipped to make a decision as valid as the parents working together might make.

New Jersey child-custody decisions should be made with the "best interests of the parties' children" in mind. But let's backtrack for just a second and define child custody in New Jersey.

### TYPES OF CUSTODY

Under New Jersey Law, there are two basic types of child custody—legal and physical. Legal custody includes the right to make important decisions regarding the children such as important decisions involving their health, religious upbringing, and education. Physical custody assigns with which parent the children will reside the majority of the time and thus who will have the day-to-day care of the children.

New Jersey law favors joint legal custody, whereas joint physical custody is generally the more contested issue. In recent years, disputes about joint physical custody have increased, and some judges start with the baseline of fifty-fifty shared joint and legal custody and ask why that ratio should change.

Often, the noncustodial party will be granted a significant amount of parenting time. The amount of overnight parenting time also plays a role in determining child-support awards.

## GENDER AND CUSTODY

New Jersey has largely become gender blind when determining custody (except perhaps when a child is very young). That said, for a variety of reasons, women are still more often granted physical custody of the children. It should be noted, however, that the number of fathers being granted primary physical custody of their children appears to be increasing. As noted above, joint custody is increasingly being expected and awarded except in exceptional circumstances.

## MODIFICATION OF NEW JERSEY CHILD-CUSTODY DECISIONS

New Jersey child-custody decisions are always subject to review and modification based on the best interests of the children. In most cases, divorcing parties consent to custody agreements in conjunction with their divorce proceedings. Until a child is an adult, however, custody issues may persist, and they can be revisited upon either party's request.

## LITIGATION OF CHILD-CUSTODY ISSUES IN NEW JERSEY

If the parties cannot resolve their custody issues, the matter will likely have to be litigated. As part of the child-support litigation, there will likely be outside experts called in to assist the court in determining what living arrangements are in the best interests of the children. Issues of parental fitness will play a larger role than the preference of the child particularly if the child is younger as I mentioned earlier.

That phrase in the block quote on previous pages, "But no stranger in a judicial robe ..." means that the court will likely push both parties toward mediation. New Jersey child-custody cases are highly fact sensitive. As such, the effective and aggressive use of all appropriate discovery techniques will be considered in contested or potentially contested custody disputes.

### *NEWBURGH V. ARRIGO FACTORS*

One particular case, the *Newburgh v. Arrigo* case, provided certain factors for courts to consider when requiring one or both parents to contribute to their child's college costs:

1.  Whether the parent, if still living with the child, would have contributed toward the costs of the requested higher education.
2.  The effect of the background, values, and goals of the parent on the reasonableness of the expectation of the child for higher education.
3.  The amount of the contribution needed for the child to pursue higher education.
4.  The ability of the parent to pay that cost.

5. The relationship of the requested contribution to the kind of school or course of study the child is seeking.
6. The parents' financial resources.
7. The commitment to and the aptitude of the child for further education.
8. The child's financial resources including assets owned or held in custodianship or trust.
9. The ability of the child to earn income during the school year or on vacation.
10. The availability of financial aid such as college grants and loans.
11. The child's relationship to the paying parent including mutual affection and shared goals as well as responsiveness to parental advice and guidance.
12. The relationship of the education requested to any prior training and to the child's long-range goals.

As you can see, there is thus no bright-line rule requiring or not requiring contribution but rather a number of factors all which must be weighed by the courts when it comes to determining what might be fair. This situation creates the somewhat interesting scenario in which divorcing couples in New Jersey might be required to contribute to their children's college costs while couples who are not divorced aren't required to do so. Some have argued that that isn't fair in that it treats one class of citizens different from another, and that might trigger constitutional issues.

The factors in *Newburgh v. Arrigo* have been around and effective for well over thirty years now, and that can prompt courts to require payment for or at least contributions to law school, medical school, or other professional school costs particularly from parents with big net worths.

## CONTRIBUTING TO A CHILD'S GAP YEAR

I've also seen courts require payments for what's called a child's gap year, a year in between high school and college or a year between this or that year of college meant as a time for travel or volunteering here or there. The courts don't consider this as a sign of emancipation as young people taking gap years generally intend to continue their education.

## EMANCIPATION AND CHILD COSTS

Other difficult factors for you to consider may be how you can prove a child is emancipated because he or she is not pursuing an education full time or in good faith and is thus no longer entitled to child support. Some clients have told me that their children are failing most classes, are taking six years to complete a four-year degree, and so on. Those cases can become difficult to prove particularly if the noncustodial parent has a strained relationship with his or her child, and it makes for interesting emancipation arguments in court.

## PARENTAL STRAIN AND COLLEGE COSTS

Finally, the issue of parent/child strain is considered in the *Newburgh v. Arrigo* factors and is an important concept. It is difficult to imagine paying for a child's education when that child won't even speak to you, but if courts determine you are more to blame for such strain than your adult child, you might be forced to do so anyway.

## PARENTING-TIME LAW IN NEW JERSEY

Parenting time—formerly referred to as visitation—addresses the specifics of a custody order or agreement. The parties' lawyers will do their best to broker a deal or fight for the parenting time sought by their clients. Likewise, judges will make a call if they have to. But in my opinion, the parties themselves are best equipped to work out the most reasonable parenting-time arrangement on a day-to-day and hour-to-hour basis. After all, they will be the ones implementing the parenting-time arrangement into the fabric of their daily lives.

Accordingly, the parties should recognize and work together to protect the best interests of their children. Ideally, they will push aside their differences and work toward a fair resolution of the parenting-time issue. As stated above, New Jersey parenting-time law itself is grounded in the belief that no "stranger in a black robe" is better equipped to resolve such matters than the parties themselves.

## BASIC CONCEPTS OF NEW JERSEY PARENTING TIME

Custody will determine which party is the parent of primary residence (physical custody) and which party is the parent of alternate residence. New Jersey law generally favors liberal parenting time with the parent of alternate residence so that the children will maintain a post-divorce relationship with both parents.

Exceptions to this general rule do exist such as when parenting time would not be in the best interests of the children. One such instance is when the parent of primary residence has a history of abuse or domestic violence. Even then, however, the courts generally favor restrictions on parenting time (such as requiring that parenting time be supervised) to denying either party parenting time altogether.

One of the seminal New Jersey parenting time cases is *McCown v. McCown*.[3] The ruling stated that children have a right to a loving relationship with both parents. The parent of primary residence generally has a responsibility to foster and develop the relationship between the children and their other parent. The parent of primary residence may therefore be sanctioned if he or she attempts to alienate the children from their other parent. Such sanctions can include up to the loss of primary custody.

Parenting-time rights are generally guaranteed only to the actual parents or guardians. Outside parties generally have no legal right to parenting time even when those outside parties are nonguardian grandparents. Parenting time is not contingent on the payment of child support.

## PARENTING-TIME AGREEMENTS

In New Jersey, parenting-time arrangements may be determined by the agreement of the parties or by the court. Either way, this issue has to be decided based on the best interests of the children.

Most courts and family law attorneys will look to a traditional parenting-time arrangement to provide a basic framework for parenting time. Negotiations will then focus on modifying the agreement to reflect the wishes of the parties. The parent of alternate residence is generally given alternate weekends for

---

3    277 <u>N.J.Super.</u> 213, 218 (App. Div. 1994).

overnights along with an evening or two each week. Fights over specific holidays can oftentimes hold up an otherwise done deal.

Holidays are generally alternated between both parents based on even and odd years. The parties can enter into an agreement for parenting time/custody as part of the Marital Settlement Agreement or as an independent Consent Order prior to the ultimate disposition of the case. This agreement would then be embodied and/or incorporated into the Marital Settlement Agreement.

## MODIFYING PARENTING-TIME AGREEMENTS

Either party may at essentially any time move for a modification of a parenting-time arrangement. If the parties cannot agree on a post-judgment modification, the party seeking the modification will often file a motion showing that there has been a significant change in circumstances and that the modification would be in the best interests of the children.

Parenting-time issues can be one of the most contentious parts of a divorce. Luckily, in many instances, the parties can work together to create an amicable resolution of their issues.

## WHO DECIDES THE CHILD'S RELIGIOUS UPBRINGING?

In a New Jersey divorce and particularly one with young children, the following questions may arise.

- Should the children be raised in a particular faith or religion?
- If yes, how active should the children be in that religion?

- Should the children attend religious education?
- If so, what if that interferes with the parenting schedule?

For example, in a divorce in which the mother is Jewish and the father is Catholic, if the parents agree to raise the child Catholic, should the mother be required to take the children to CCD classes during her parenting time? Should the parents agree to split the costs of religious education? Should the mother in the above example be required to help pay for her children's holy communion luncheon or confirmation dinner?

How often should the children attend religious ceremonies? For instance, should a parent be required to attend church or synagogue with the children even if they are not of the same faith?

If the parents agree on raising a child in a specific faith, to what extent do they agree or not regarding parochial or private school in that religion versus public school?

## THE ROLE OF COURTS IN DETERMINING NEW JERSEY DIVORCE RELIGIOUS CHOICE ISSUES

In New Jersey, most parties have joint legal custody at the time that they divorce; both are supposed to have a say in determining important issues of education, religion, health, and the like regarding their children. This can present a unique challenge when a stalemate arises between the parties.

For instance, in the above classic example of a Jewish mother and a Catholic father, they may have a newborn and have not decided in which faith their child will be raised. If they decide to divorce, that issue can rise to the surface. If they can't agree, the court will be called upon to do so, but the court abhors nothing more than deciding such religious questions. First Amendment and other constitutional issues are at play, judges are loath to make any decision that might make it look as if they're preferring one religion to another, and the court recognizes that for any type of plan to work, it will likely require buy-in by *both* parents.

Courts may punt this issue entirely. They can state that the children shall be raised in both faiths, or they might take no position on this issue at all. If the parties have a parenting coordinator, perhaps he or she might assist them, and mediation may help, but if not, what can be done?

Some guidelines that parties may wish to consider in such an instance may include these.

- how religious or not each party is
- the religious backgrounds of the parents' families
- the importance of the issue to each party
- which parent will be more committed to the responsibilities associated with raising children in his or her faith
- what steps have already been taken to raise the child in a specific faith
- if other children of the relationship have been baptized or otherwise been raised in a specific faith
- to what extent both parties are acting in good faith in raising such issues
- to what extent the parenting plan allows for the children to be raised in a specific faith; if there is a language component to a specific religion or faith, how the parenting schedule will allow the children to learn the language to meet religious requirements

It will ultimately be very much up to the parties in such circumstances to put aside any animosity they may have toward each other and cooperate in the best interests of their children to reach a conclusion in this matter.

## WHO PROVIDES HEALTH INSURANCE AND UNREIMBURSED MEDICAL EXPENSES FOR THE CHILDREN?

During a marriage, it is common for one party to provide health insurance for the whole family. For instance, my wife works for a school district, and her policy covers our whole family.

In divorces, courts strive to preserve the *status quo* of the marriage, so prior to the divorce being finalized, the party who has always provided health insurance should continue to do so.

That party should also pay out-of-pocket expenses following any *pendente lite* (court orders in place during pendency of divorce proceedings) orders.

## WHAT ABOUT AFTER A DIVORCE IS FINALIZED?

In New Jersey, the Divorce Agreement should set forth all the obligations of both parties concerning who pays for ongoing health insurance and out-of-pocket expenses.

## HEALTH INSURANCE COVERAGE FOR A SPOUSE

The obligation of one spouse to maintain health insurance for the other ends the day the divorce is finalized. Even if you wish to maintain your spouse on your policy, most workplace or other health insurance policies won't allow that. The most one can do is offer the other spouse COBRA insurance, the cost for which is generally paid to the spouse who lacks health insurance. COBRA insurance can generally last up to eighteen months. The finalizing of a divorce generally requires both parties to start maintaining their own health insurance policies.

## HEALTH INSURANCE COVERAGE FOR CHILDREN

The Divorce Agreement should set forth which parent will maintain health insurance for the children. The cost of this and any out-of-pocket costs should be figured into the amount of child support one parent pays. The agreement may establish what is to happen if one parent loses his or her health insurance. If neither party has health insurance, the agreement may set forth the actions they are to take to obtain health insurance and the division of any costs as applicable.

## UNREIMBURSED MEDICAL EXPENSES FOR CHILDREN

The Divorce Agreement should also set forth how unreimbursed medical expenses will be handled. Under general New Jersey law, the parent of primary residence is responsible for the first $250 each year per child, and the parties thereafter will divide any additional out-of-pocket costs such as copays, for braces and dental work, or other out-of-network or out-of-pocket expenses.

The parties may agree to divide the costs beyond the first $250 each year per child evenly or in some other ratio depending on their incomes. The parties may also include language in the Divorce Agreement that handles additional details; they could agree that they'll both try to stay in-network except in emergencies, that they'll keep each other informed about any medical issues, that proof of out-of-pocket expenses will be shown in a timely fashion, and so on.

## CONCLUSION

The above issues are fact sensitive and should be considered as part of any divorce settlement as applicable. As medical expenses become an increasingly important consideration, those who are contemplating, negotiating, or finalizing a New Jersey divorce should keep these issues in mind.

# CHAPTER 16

# *New Jersey Alimony*

Alimony can be one of the thorniest issues in a New Jersey divorce. It's often the most difficult issue to negotiate in cases in which the parties have no children. The New Jersey Alimony Reform Statute and recent changes to the federal tax code have made alimony even more difficult to calculate.

## ALIMONY DEFINED

Alimony—also referred to as spousal support—involves one of the parties in a divorce paying the other enough to equitably preserve the marital lifestyle between the parties post-marriage.

The standard type of alimony case initially considered by the court was the situation in which one spouse had put everything into his or her career and earned a large salary while the other had stayed home to raise the children and had a deflated earning potential at the time of their divorce. Alimony has now grown to be more prevalent than perhaps initially intended but was recently scaled back some by alimony reform.

Let's consider a few alimony scenarios that will help us see New Jersey alimony through a number of prisms and better understand how it can affect people in the real world. People tend to have strong opinions about alimony, but the below examples should point out that alimony is a difficult matter from a moral as well as a legal perspective.

## HISTORY OF ALIMONY

According to Wikipedia (so it must be true!), alimony and child support are discussed in writing as far back as the Code of Hammurabi.

> The modern concept of alimony is derived from English Ecclesiastical courts that awarded alimony in cases of separation and divorce. *Alimony pendente lite* was given until the divorce decree, based on the husband's duty to support the wife during a marriage that still continued. *Post-divorce* or *permanent alimony* was also based on the notion that the marriage continued, as ecclesiastical courts could only award a *divorce a mensa et thoro*, similar to a legal separation today. As divorce did not end the marriage, the husband's duty to support his wife remained intact.

So alimony is an ancient idea that became increasingly important in the 1970s as the divorce rate peaked.

## ALIMONY EXAMPLES

### THE CLASSIC EXAMPLE

In what we'll call the classic alimony scenario, imagine Sarah and Sam. Sarah has a master's degree in teaching and spent eight years teaching second grade.

When Sarah's and Sam's first child was born, they decided she would give up teaching to take care of their child. Sam had recently moved up in his company, and they were able to live comfortably off his income. They wanted another child, and they figured that child-care costs for the two children would exceed what Sarah could earn as a teacher.

Fifteen years later, Sam, a vice president at his company, was earning $200,000 a year. Sarah went back to teaching as a preschool teacher and was earning $20,000 per year. Unfortunately, their relationship deteriorated and Sarah filed for divorce. Had Sarah remained working at the school all those years, she would have been earning $100,000 per year at that point and looking forward to a nice pension they'd both share in retirement.

Is it appropriate for Sarah to expect alimony so she can live a life close to what she had lived with Sam? Could one argue that perhaps a middle ground is appropriate? Maybe Sarah should receive alimony for a certain number of years with the expectation that she will find gainful employment again? If you're in the middle of a separation or contemplating divorce, can you relate to Sarah or Sam?

## A MORE MODERN EXAMPLE

We'll call this the modern alimony scenario. Jill and Jim have been married for twenty-two years. Jim has worked in construction his entire career and earns $125,000 per year. Jill built up an interior design company that now employs five people, and she nets approximately $125,000 per year. Jim has ongoing back issues but never complains—they are likely caused by his job, but he doesn't seek workers' compensation.

One day, Jim gets called in and is told his company is letting him go because management is unhappy with his work performance. Jim, however, suspects that his company wants to hire two younger people to replace his one salary. Jim is given a few months' severance pay and attempts to find a job while he collects unemployment.

Eventually, his unemployment benefits run out, and he hasn't found a job. He begins drinking heavily and becomes depressed. Jill tries to make it work and even increases her income to $150,000, but eventually, their relationship deteriorates and she files for divorce.

Should Jill have to pay alimony to Jim? How much? For how many years? And how much income if any should be imputed to each of them? Should Jim be imputed income based on his prior income, his current situation, or somewhere in between? Should Jill be imputed income based on an average of her business income, her recent higher salary, or $125,000 per year?

## DIFFERENCES BETWEEN ALIMONY AND CHILD SUPPORT

There is no definitive alimony calculation or calculator under New Jersey law as there is for child support, and child support ultimately ends. On the other hand, alimony must be defined not only regarding the amount paid but also the duration of the payments. Calculating alimony is more an art than a science.

One party to a divorce can waive any right to alimony; some who might have otherwise been entitled to alimony might agree to a lump-sum payment for instance and be in a sense bought out. But unlike alimony, child support cannot be waived by a parent because the law considers child support as a right belonging to the child. Child-support money goes to one parent, but it is meant for the benefit of the children, not him or her. If you agree to waive child support, that could come back to haunt you in the form of retroactive payment obligations.

## DURATION OF ALIMONY

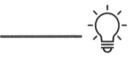

Though the alimony statute, other relevant statutes, and case law have a more global view, in a practical sense, generally only the last one to five years of a divorcing couple's finances will determine the length alimony will be paid.

That means that when you file for divorce could be very important in terms of how much alimony you might receive and for how long you'll receive it. If you're filing for divorce when your spouse's income is at an all-time low, that could affect how much alimony you receive and

**If you agree to waive child support, that could come back to haunt you in the form of retroactive payment obligations.**

in some cases greatly. In addition, overtime and bonuses may be considered in New Jersey divorce actions.

As with Jill in our hypothetical scenario above, an individual's recent success can end up harming the outcome of his or her case. If Jill filed for divorce at the time she and Jim were both earning $125,000 per year, neither party would have likely had to pay alimony. But because she waited to file until a few years later when Jim was completely unemployed and she was earning $150,000, Jim's attorney would likely argue that she has a large alimony obligation, and then Jill's attorney would have to argue that their most recent financial history doesn't give a good picture of their total financial history and the marital lifestyle they enjoyed.

## DURATION OF ALIMONY—JIM AND JILL ANALYSIS

Is that a fair result? If the recent *status quo* for a hypothetical couple was for one party to work eighty hours a week and the other to work part-time (even though he or she was healthy and free to work full-time), is it fair that alimony will often be based on their recent earnings and W-2s?

What if the party working part time simply has no desire to work or knows he or she can later rely upon a huge inheritance? What if the party working part time has a higher level of education and a greater ability to earn income than the party working eighty hours a week? To use another example, what if one party's salary is on an upward trajectory—how can that be factored into create a fair starting point for alimony and child support?

Conversely, is it too nebulous a proposition for courts to focus more on all the alimony factors? Or is it understood that focusing on merely the last year (or two or three) may be somewhat flawed but that there is no better way to cleanly resolve such issues?

I'd never suggest that people should try to game the system, neglect maintaining the *status quo*, or start turning down all overtime work if they feel separation or divorce is imminent because such divorce "planning" can be detrimental to a case and in some instances particularly those involving hiding of assets may even be illegal.

Rather, I wish to illuminate how the timing of a relationship's ending can be just as important a factor as the end achieved by divorce and an MSA. This is because the facts associated with a relationship's ending (particularly when a formal divorce pleading is filed) may affect more than any other single factor the ultimate disposition of a case.

## OPEN-DURATIONAL ALIMONY

A good rule of thumb is that a party is responsible for paying one year of alimony for every two years of marriage. You won't find this anywhere on the books but as a matter of custom. It's a rule of thumb most New Jersey divorce lawyers use as a sort of shorthand for alimony. In addition, under the Alimony Reform Statute of 2014, the statute states that alimony is open durational alimony, which was once called permanent alimony, once the parties are married for twenty years.

## ALIMONY AND GOOD-FAITH RETIREMENT

The alimony statute also states that there is a rebuttable presumption that alimony will end when the party responsible for alimony reaches "good-faith retirement," which is generally defined as a person reaching the age at which he or she can claim full Social Security retirement benefits. Accordingly, this will depend on what year you were born as the younger you are, the older you will have to be to qualify.

The court will then review factors to determine if the conditions for good-faith retirement have been met. The law states as follows.

1. It is presumed (though this could be argued) that alimony should end when the spouse receiving alimony reaches full retirement age (but any alimony owed—missed past payments—at

that point still has to be paid). The court may end alimony at a different date if it determines there's a good reason to do so based on a number of considerations including the following.

- the ages of the parties at the time of the application for retirement
- the ages of the parties at the time of the marriage or civil union and their ages at the time of entry of the alimony award
- The degree and duration of the economic dependency of the recipient upon the payor during the marriage or civil union.
- whether the recipient has forgone or relinquished or otherwise sacrificed claims, rights, or property in exchange for a more substantial or longer alimony award
- the duration or amount of alimony already paid
- the health of the parties at the time of the retirement application
- assets of the parties at the time of the retirement application
- whether the recipient has reached full retirement age
- sources of income both earned and unearned of the parties
- the ability of the recipient to have saved adequately for retirement
- any other factors the court deems relevant.

## CAN I WAIVE ALIMONY?

It is common for a party to be entitled to some form of alimony at the time of divorce even now with post-alimony reform. Alimony in New Jersey is viewed as gender neutral; if the wife had been the breadwinner, she may be required to pay alimony to the husband.

Some of the types of standard alimony factors considered include the income levels of the parties, whether additional income may be imputed based on prior education or experience, the age and health of the parties, what the marital standard of living had been, and the length of the marriage.

Someone can waive his or her right to receive alimony provided that the Marital Settlement Agreement was freely and fairly entered into and contains certain language known as *anti-lepis* language stating that that person permanently waives any rights to alimony and that that agreement cannot be changed under any circumstances.

There are many valid reasons for someone to waive alimony. Some consider it a point of pride or a moral issue; others might do so due to guilty feelings for having, say, had an affair. Others might be looking for a quick divorce and are willing to leave money on the table to speed up the process and minimize its legal costs. Some people who were victims of domestic violence might simply be afraid to ask for alimony.

Regardless of the reason for someone waiving alimony, the court will bind consenting adults to their contractual agreements. Those wanting to receive or waive alimony or thinking about offering or accepting an alimony buyout offer should weigh all the factors carefully because what they decide will have an effect on their future.

Any waiver of alimony should include what's called "Crews" language (in addition to the *anti-lepis* language I mentioned just above) that notes the marital lifestyle during the marriage and the impact the divorce will have on the parties' lifestyles after their divorce; this should be standard in every MSA.

**Be very careful about waiving alimony as it can be difficult or impossible to change that even if your circumstances later change and you decide you need alimony. This is just one area of the divorce process for which you will really need a lawyer's advice. This is particularly the case, as I mentioned, when you feel emotionally drained and just want to finalize a divorce. You don't want to make a rash decision you'll later end up regretting**

## NEW JERSEY ALIMONY REFORM ACT

The New Jersey legislature enacted the Alimony Reform Act in 2014. The basic factors judges will consider when determining an alimony award may now include:

1. the actual need and ability of the parties to pay
2. the duration of the marriage
3. the age, physical, and emotional health of the parties
4. the standard of living established in the marriage and the likelihood that each party can maintain a reasonably comparable standard of living
5. the earning capacities, educational levels, vocational skills, and employability of the parties

6. the length of absence from the job market and custodial responsibilities for children of the party seeking maintenance

7. parental responsibilities for any children

8. the time and expense necessary to acquire sufficient education or training to enable the party seeking maintenance to find appropriate employment, the availability of the training and employment, and the opportunity for future acquisitions of capital assets and income

9. the history of the financial or nonfinancial contributions to the marriage by each party including contributions to the care and education of the children and interruption of personal careers or educational opportunities

10. the equitable distribution of property ordered and any payout of equitable distribution, directly or indirectly, from current income, to the extent that this consideration is reasonable, just, and fair

11. the income available to either party through investments of all assets held by the party

12. the tax treatment and consequences to both parties of any alimony awards

13. the nature, amount, and length of *pendente lite* support paid if any

14. any other factors the court deems relevant.

Okay, but what does the above really mean? How will these factors coalesce into an alimony award assuming an alimony award is appropriate at all?

When I explain alimony reform to new clients, I generally do not focus on the above factors. The truth is that those factors do not form the heart of real-life alimony negotiations. Instead, I believe those new to the concept of alimony should focus on the following.

## ALIMONY IS LEGALLY SPEAKING NOW GENDER NEUTRAL

Although we may not have reached 100 percent gender neutrality, we're getting closer. As I mentioned, if the wife is the breadwinner in a long-term marriage, she may expect to pay alimony.

## THE LENGTH OF THE MARRIAGE IS EXTREMELY IMPORTANT

There are different types of alimony that may be awarded in New Jersey including open-durational alimony (formerly called permanent alimony as mentioned). There is also rehabilitative alimony, limited-duration alimony, and reimbursement alimony discussed at greater length below. Permanent alimony for those divorced prior to the reform continues.

For obvious reasons, most breadwinners want to avoid paying long-standing or open-durational alimony. The longer the parties are married, however, the greater the chances are that one will be faced with a financial burden. This is particularly true with marriages that exceed twenty years though there is no hard and fast rule to determine whether alimony should be open durational. The alimony reform statute does state, however, that "For any marriage or civil union less than twenty years in duration, the total duration of alimony shall not, except in exceptional circumstances, exceed the length of the marriage or civil union."

The factors for "exceptional circumstances" for an award to last longer than the marriage include these.

1. the age of the parties at the time of the marriage or civil union and at the time of the alimony award
2. the degree and duration of the dependency of one party on the other
3. whether a spouse or partner has a chronic illness or unusual health circumstances
4. whether a spouse or partner has given up a career
5. whether a spouse or partner has received a disproportionate share of equitable distribution
6. the impact of the marriage or civil union on either party's ability to become self-supporting
7. tax considerations
8. any other relevant factors

**Alimony was historically taxable to the recipient and deductible to the payer, but not any longer** since the changes to the tax code. The parties can agree to a buyout of alimony rather than it going on for years, but the tax consequences of that have not been settled. There may be an obligation to provide life insurance as a form of security for the alimony due.

## GOOD-FAITH RETIREMENT, COHABITATION, AND REMARRIAGE

These additional factors may provide sufficient reasons to terminate, suspend, or modify alimony. Assuming there is no language to the contrary, permanent and substantial changes in circumstances may also provide reasons to amend and in some instances even terminate an existing alimony obligation.

The Alimony Reform Act made substantial changes to cohabitation and particularly to good-faith retirement including the creation of the presumption I mentioned that alimony should end when the person paying it reaches a good-faith, full retirement age. As mentioned, other factors could affect this including the ages of the parties when alimony started, the degree and duration of economic dependency, the duration of alimony or what's already been paid, and current sources of income.

## PROTECTING ALIMONY

Life insurance will also often play a role in protecting alimony. For instance, if the Marital Settlement Agreement grants the husband $1,000 a month in alimony for ten years, the wife should be required to get a life insurance policy that will cover the total amount, $120,000. That policy could be reduced as the years go on.

## HOW THE TAX CUT AND JOBS ACT OF 2018 AFFECTED ALIMONY

The Trump Tax Reform Act of 2018 made several changes to New Jersey divorce law including making alimony a tax-neutral event. The Federal Tax and Jobs Act modified alimony so that it was no longer taxable as of January 1, 2019. The person receiving alimony won't have that taxed, and the person paying alimony will not be able to deduct it.

As the person paying alimony is generally in a higher tax bracket, this change was made at the federal level to support some of the tax deductions as part of the tax act.

There is now some confusion; divorce attorneys and judges will have to learn how to calculate the effect of taxes on Divorce Agreements so that neither party receives an unfair advantage. Individuals will likely pay less alimony, but it will be the same as they would have paid prior to the changes as it will no longer be tax deductible.

Most *pendente lite* alimony awards are unallocated or mixed with child-support payments and have therefore generally been tax neutral.

Currently (subject to a phase-out) parents may receive a tax credit of $1,000 per child. The Tax Reform Act doubled that amount to $2,000. In divorces, the child tax credits are generally evenly divided between the parties. Accordingly, if there are two unemancipated children from a marriage, both parents will claim one. If there is one child, the parents will alternate even and odd years claiming the children. I like to add language to my Divorce Agreements that if a parent cannot benefit from a deduction in a given year that they will allow the other parent to claim the child. This provision increases the value of child tax credits and instantly makes it twice as important a consideration for future divorces.

## STATE AND LOCAL TAX DEDUCTIONS AND PROPERTY TAXES

Those who reside in New Jersey don't need me to remind them we're a heavily taxed state with high property values and high property taxes as well, but how does that affect couples seeking a divorce in the state? For one thing, many experts are forecasting that home values may be reduced particularly for properties with $10,000 or more in property taxes. Just as many people attempted to prepay their property taxes before the changes went into effect, there may be more people considering filing for divorce before the values of their homes decrease. For most individuals their largest single asset is their home. If their home decreases in value, so does the marital pot for purposes of equitable distribution. Thus this too requires careful monitoring particularly as we enter the post-holiday divorce season.

## PRENUPS AND ALIMONY

So many people are eligible to receive alimony in different forms. Generally, the greater the disparity in income between the parties and the longer their marriage, the more alimony one will have to pay to the other.

A prenuptial agreement may call for a permanent waiver of alimony. If that's the case, it's important to recognize what your expected benefit from receiving alimony could be before you agree to waive it. We cannot predict the future, but we can think about what might be out there in the future, and any prenup should take that into consideration as best it can.

There's no requirement that a prenup be fair; it just cannot be what's called "unconscionable" at the time the agreement is signed. Accordingly, those getting married should consider whether a prenuptial agreement makes sense, and those getting divorced should get advice on whether their existing prenups are indeed enforceable and to what extent they can affect alimony.

## ALIMONY STANDARD

The general burden of proof is on the party seeking alimony or seeking to modify an alimony amount. The law in such cases looks into whether the person receiving alimony will be able to maintain a lifestyle reasonably comparable to that enjoyed during the marriage itself.[4]

## WHAT ARE MY RESPONSIBILITIES WHILE THE DIVORCE IS PENDING?

Essentially, while the divorce is pending (the *pendente lite* phase of litigation), both parties are to maintain the marital status quo—keeping insurance policies paid up, not spending wildly or otherwise dissipating marital assets, not taking on inappropriate marital debt, paying regular expenses, and the like. If the husband normally pays the mortgage and the wife pays the car notes, that practice should continue. Parenting time and access to children should also maintain the status quo of the marriage.

Unlike other areas of the law that involve singular events such as an automobile accident, divorce law is a moving picture, not a snapshot in that people have to continue living their lives as the divorce is ongoing. Temporary parenting time, custody, child support, and yes, alimony may be ordered *pendente lite* or agreed to between the parties by consent, but that will stop after the divorce is finalized. *Pendente lite* support may be combined with child support and is generally made without prejudice, meaning that an overpayment of *pendente lite* support may later be reimbursed at the time the divorce is finalized.

Occasionally, circumstances will change such as one party leaving the marital residence. In such circumstances, the court will view the available money for each party and attempt to equalize that amount.

Courts take the marital lifestyle quite literally. Case law states that even if the parties have been living beyond their

---

4    An important case on this subject is Crews v. Crews, 164 N.J. 11, 16 (2000).

means and are going increasingly into debt, during the *pendente lite* phase of the litigation, they can continue to do so. So in the example of Jim and Jill, the court would likely require Jill to continue making all marital payments or send a sum of money to Jim every month if he moved out of the martial residence in an attempt to continue the *status quo* of the marital lifestyle.

One of the most important parts of a contested New Jersey divorce is making sure you minimize or maximize depending on whether you are the paying or receiving spouse of the *pendente lite* amount. That will take away the other side's ability to maneuver during the actual divorce negotiations. For instance, if Jim's attorney doesn't file an appropriate *pendente lite* motion or does not broker a deal and Jim is left in an apartment with minimal income, he might be quick to settle for a lesser amount than he would otherwise be entitled to. For this reason, I often see a great deal of gamesmanship with parties filling out their Case Information Statements that set forth the Schedules A, B, and C that deal with the marital lifestyle.

## ALIMONY AT TRIAL

In New Jersey, each county has a superior court. If your divorce is in Hunterdon County for example, your alimony claim will be heard in that county's superior court.

Alimony can be negotiated at any time between the parties. However, if the parties cannot negotiate an amount, the superior court judge will have to make the call for the parties regarding the amount and duration of alimony. The court may rely upon experts (as discussed above), testimony, and a review of evidentiary records to determine the appropriate alimony award. Consistent with case law,[5] the marital lifestyle will be determined, income will be found or imputed, and a baseline for future alimony motions will be created.

Certain cases[6] state that the trial court's decision should be based on the actual lifestyle rather than what the parties' lifestyle should have been based on their income, assets, and marital debts. The parties can also agree to a buyout, or the court could order a buyout or the liquidation of certain marital assets to satisfy an alimony obligation.

## A QUICK NOTE ON EXEMPT PROPERTY

Certain types of property are generally exempt (unless they've been commingled) during a New Jersey divorce including inherited property, gifted property, premarital property, and a portion of personal injury or worker's comp.

Things get interesting when exempt property is involved. For instance, in the Jim and Jill example, if Jim had taken worker's comp and received approximately 70 percent of his income and the parties divorced during that time, how would that be treated for purposes of alimony?

If Jim's salary was then effectively $87,500 versus Jill's $125,000, he would be imputed income at $87,500 or a lesser amount because by law, the portion of a workers' comp award for pain and suffering is not subject to division in a divorce. Conversely, the portion attributable to lost wages (likely the majority of the award) would be subject to division, and the same is true for personal-injury awards.

---

5    Crews v. Crews, and Lepis v. Lepis, 83 N.J. 139 (1980).

6    Including *Weishaus v. Weishaus*, 360 N.J. Super. 281 (App. Div. 2003).

As you can see, there can be a lot of interesting arguments made regarding the appropriate alimony award when issues of exempt property or exempt earnings (and any income, debt, or interest coming from that) enter the picture.

## SUPERSEDING ALIMONY TERMINATION EVENTS

Most divorce decrees state that alimony will terminate upon the end date of alimony as negotiated between the parties or when the payee remarries or dies or when the payor dies. Alimony can be renegotiated (but generally not terminated) if the payee cohabitates with another adult in a romantic partnership that provides economic support or advantage to the payee.

Rest assured that you won't generally be required to continue paying alimony after you die. The Divorce Agreement will likely kick in making your spouse whole with the proceeds from a life insurance policy.

Once alimony is terminated, it generally cannot be reinstated. If, say, it ends when your ex remarries, if you ex then divorces, he or she can't come after you to start up the alimony again (unless perhaps that marriage is annulled a week after it happened, but case law doesn't cover that possibility—yet).

## TYPES OF ALIMONY

In most instances the question of alimony will be whether a party should receive open-duration or limited-duration alimony. In either instance alimony may be terminated by certain events even if it's open-duration alimony.

The types of alimony available are by statute, and they were affected by the New Jersey Tax Reform Act of 2014.

## LIMITED-DURATIONAL ALIMONY

For New Jersey marriages that last less than twenty years, the parties will generally negotiate limited-durational alimony. For instance, with a sixteen-year marriage, the parties may agree to limited-duration alimony of eight years.

## OPEN-DURATIONAL ALIMONY

This is the type of alimony that replaced what was previously called permanent alimony prior to the New Jersey Alimony Reform Act of 2014. It is somewhat softer than permanent alimony in that it allows for a rebuttable presumption of alimony termination along with a good-faith retirement as was addressed above.

## REHABILITATIVE ALIMONY

Rehabilitative alimony is less common than open-durational alimony or limited-durational alimony. This type of alimony is meant to help an ex obtain education, update credentials, or take other steps to become self-supporting or more self-supporting. This type of alimony may be ordered in lieu of the other types of alimony, or it may work in tandem with open-durational or limited-durational alimony. In some cases, open-durational alimony has been ordered after rehabilitative alimony ended.

For example, in the Sarah and Sam example above, Sarah might receive rehabilitative alimony to pay for additional coursework or credentials to become a fully licensed teacher again and increase her income. It might be agreed that once she's earning $50,000 per year, the court will order additional alimony to reflect the difference between her income and Sam's.

## CAN FAULT IMPACT AN ALIMONY AWARD?

Because New Jersey is a no-fault divorce state, matters such as adultery should make no difference regarding alimony award. That's not to say adultery won't make a difference in custody or parenting-time arguments, but courts are not allowed under the case law[7] to increase, decrease, or otherwise affect alimony based on the behavior of one spouse toward the other.

That said, courts can determine someone's at fault should that person's actions or inactions intentionally impact alimony. People can't legally quit paying alimony and child support if they quit their jobs, get jailed for a crime, or intentionally try to reduce or hide their income.

In Jill and Jim's example, if Jim lost his job because he was caught drinking while operating a forklift or if he deliberately waited to file for divorce for a time when he was out of work, that wouldn't have a place in an alimony calculation but in a much more specific manner—courts could impute income if they believe a party is intentionally unemployed or underemployed.

If you are out of a job during a divorce or post-divorce, document all your attempts to find a new job. Save copies of your applications and log the hours you spend on job boards, networking, increasing your skills, interviewing, and applying for jobs. This will help you if the other party tries to convince the court that you're intentionally unemployed, underemployed, or otherwise attempting to game the alimony system.

If the other party physically harmed you, you could have a marital tort claim,[8] which is similar to any other type of personal-injury action and would involve fault, but is not truly a

---

7    See cases such as Mani v. Mani, 183 N.J. 70.

8    under cases such as *Tevis v. Tevis.*

form of alimony. A marital tort is meant to pay for actual harm whereas alimony is meant to replace income or otherwise ensure both parties can continue to enjoy lifestyles reasonably similar to what they had during their marriage.

In sum, the concept of fault in a divorce will generally affect alimony only when that fault has affected finances such as causing your spouse to lose a job, intentionally losing your job, or otherwise attempting to game the system to pay less or receive more alimony than you're entitled to.

## MODIFYING ALIMONY

Parties can negotiate whether alimony will be nonmodifiable—if it can be increased, decreased, suspended, terminated, or otherwise modified based upon a "permanent and substantial change in circumstances." Courts will generally honor that clause.

The advantage to a lump-sum buyout is that the money is at less risk should either party pass away or should that spouse decide to remarry or cohabitate. Also, there is the time-value of money to be considered—the value of $1,000 a month today compared to what its value will be in ten years due to inflation and other factors. A bird in hand can beat two in the bush.

### LIMITED-DURATIONAL ALIMONY MODIFICATION

So what happens if your ex gets a great job a year after your divorce or even more wins the lottery the day after your divorce is finalized? Can you go back and seek a greater alimony amount? Maybe.

What about changing limited-durational alimony to open-durational alimony? In one case,[9] the appellate court held that a subsequent increase in earnings and career improvement by the alimony payor should generally not lead to open-durational alimony because alimony is based more on the previous marital lifestyle, not the new one a huge windfall might make possible.

## PERMANENT AND SUBSTANTIAL CHANGE IN CIRCUMSTANCES

There's no clear-cut definition of what constitutes a "substantial change" in someone's circumstances; that's decided on a case-by-case basis.

In order to modify alimony, it must be shown that a loss of income was not through the fault or was intentional on the part of the party seeking to suspend, terminate, or reduce alimony, and it's the same situation with child-support modifications.

Sometimes, clients will want to change their alimony obligation a few weeks after losing a job, but New Jersey courts have historically required a significant change that lasts for at least eighteen months and up to two years before they would consider reducing, terminating, or suspending alimony.

During the Great Recession, I clerked for a New Jersey family law judge and saw firsthand courts softening on that stand. Today, a substantial change might have to last only six months or a year to warrant in their minds a reduction in alimony

---

9    *Gordon v. Rozenwald*, 380 N.J. Super 55 (App. Div. 2005).

## PAYMENT OF ALIMONY

Alimony can be paid directly to the payee or to the Probation Department/Family Support Services. The parties' agreement will generally state how alimony will be handled and what happens if it isn't. A party seeking payment through a probation account is by law allowed to receive money in that manner. Most alimony payors do not want to pay through probation accounts, but it's not an area they can much negotiate if the other side doesn't agree.

## ALIMONY COLLECTION ISSUES

If the alimony payor stops paying alimony, the payee can petition the court to have it paid to the Probation/Family Support services. If that's already the case, the Probation Department will likely take certain steps such as suspending the payor's driver's license all the way up through temporary incarceration.

Most payment is through wage garnishment, and it's the payor's responsibility to advise the Probation Department of any employment changes or changes to his or her physical or work address. Alimony and child support are also treated as a matter of law and could result in a temporary lien on any property owned by the payor. Accordingly, if there are alimony arrears, the other party may pursue through the Family Division, not the Civil Division, enforcement actions seeking payment of arrears, having the other party turn over his or her passport until the back alimony is paid along with interest, counsel fees for liquidating property to pay it off, and any other appropriate enforcement actions somewhat similar to the collection of any other type of debt.

## HOW DOES BANKRUPTCY AFFECT A DIVORCE OR SUPPORT OBLIGATIONS?

Under bankruptcy laws, most types of debts are discharged if a successful Chapter 7 bankruptcy is completed. There are certain types of debts, however, such as student loans that are generally nondischargeable—and they include alimony. But someone who files for Chapter 13 in an attempt to renegotiate debt payments, not discharge them, could get additional time to pay back alimony and child support.

It should be noted that even equitable distribution debts are considered domestic support obligations, meaning that the bankruptcy code gives a broad interpretation to such obligations.

New Jersey bankruptcy attorneys can assist you or your divorce attorney in planning appropriate strategies regarding bankruptcy issues that will affect a pending divorce. In some instances, it may make sense to file jointly prior to the divorce and in others to file separately. This is sometimes complicated and requires a bankruptcy attorney to at least consult on the appropriate course of action.

Although the economy is in a better state that it was during the Great Recession, debt remains an important consideration for those contemplating divorce. Alimony and child support obligations can feel overwhelming to pay or to worry about not receiving. As is the case with most family law matters, the facts are critical and generally unique to each case.

# CHAPTER 17

## *Divorce Tips*

### WHAT ISSUES SHOULD A DIVORCE AGREEMENT ADDRESS?

As I've mentioned, the goal for couples divorcing in New Jersey is crafting a Marital Settlement Agreement (MSA; it's sometimes called a Property Settlement Agreement or PSA). That, however, can take months or even years though at times it can seem just barely out of reach. Some divorcing couples find common ground in a matter of hours whereas others require extensive discovery, court motions and actions, and hundreds of hours of negotiation.

In this section, I'll go over what's usually in MSAs.

### STANDARD DIVORCE AGREEMENT CONSIDERATIONS

#### *CHILD CUSTODY AND PARENTING TIME*

As mentioned earlier, if a divorcing couple has children, that will be a major divorce consideration that covers legal custody—the ability to make important decisions on behalf of the children—and physical custody—who spends more time caring for them daily. In recent years, joint physical custody is becoming more popular.

Parenting time (previously referred to as child visitation) delves more deeply into the day-to-day technical details of shared parenting. It will address drop-off and pick-up, day care, school transportation, holiday parenting time, vacation and summer parenting time, and which days/hours per week each parent will exercise parenting time with the children.

## ALIMONY

An MSA will spell out the type and amount of alimony based on a number of factors including the family's pre-divorce lifestyle, whether one spouse is the breadwinner while the other focused on raising the children and thus will probably have financial difficulties after the divorce, and a number of other factors. (See chapter 16 for an in-depth discussion of alimony.)

## CHILD SUPPORT

This is a calculation of a number of factors including with which parent the children spend most of their time.

## DIVISION OF ASSETS

The concept of assets is broad in New Jersey divorce cases. Assets may include everything from pet (yes, dogs are considered property in New Jersey) and credit card and personal debts to vehicles, the marital residence or other real estate, stock options, retirement accounts, personal items, and much more. Cases where one or both parties own a business can further complicate equitable distribution in a MSA. (See the "Business Appraisers" section in chapter 19.)

## COUNSEL FEES

Divorces can sometimes be costly and time-consuming. One thing that should be considered is whether one party should be responsible for reimbursement of counsel fees to the other.

## FUTURE EDUCATION COSTS

Another consideration is how future college costs, private school costs, or even day-care costs will be paid and the obligation each party will have to make such payments in the present or future.

## LIFE INSURANCE REQUIREMENTS

The Divorce Agreement should also address using life insurance to cover future child support, alimony, educational costs, and other future costs.

## HEALTH INSURANCE/FUTURE HEALTH COSTS

A Divorce Agreement should also contain language regarding COBRA for the uninsured spouse (generally available at cost to the uninsured spouse for eighteen months), coverage for any children of the relationship, and to what extent each party will be responsible for paying out-of-pocket medical costs.

## TAX TREATMENT

Most New Jersey divorce attorneys are not tax experts and thus cannot provide tax advice, so you should speak with a CPA or tax attorney (and coordinate this with your divorce attorney) on issues involving taxes and divorce.

## EDUCATION/CHILD'S SURNAME/RELIGIOUS UPBRINGING

The Divorce Agreement should also address potential parenting issue such as religious upbringing, education (for instance, private school or public), nondisparagement clauses regarding the other parent and his or her family, and other miscellaneous provisions.

The above list is by no means exhaustive but should provide a good framework for the types of issues that a Divorce Agreement should address.

## USING CIVIL LITIGATION TACTICS IN A HIGH-CONFLICT DIVORCE

I've said before that not many divorces turn into knock-down, drag-out events, and I generally tell my clients not to make their divorces big battles. Lawyers who consider themselves hammers tend to look at every problem as a nail that's sticking out, whack it down, and bill for that. I advise clients to avoid taking overly aggressive and ultimately pointless positions. They should be focusing on living Happily *Even* After, not seeking revenge.

Most of my clients ultimately find their ways to amicable resolutions. Perhaps neither party is completely happy with the settlement, but both calm down and realize they can live with it and move on with their lives. There's a real value to that certainty and the ability to get unstuck from a bad situation. Many of the cases I work on tend to go fairly smoothly, and there's rarely a need to take off the gloves and duke it out.

Invariably, however, some cases get so complex or driven by emotions that they require motion after motion to be filed and tougher tactics to be employed. This section of the book is all about what kinds of tactics are out there if you're contemplating a New Jersey divorce and you think it could become contentious. Some readers are probably interested in some of the more aggressive techniques they or their lawyers might need to use, so I offer here a short primer utilizing my civil litigation background.

I've always done family law, but for a time, I was deputy counsel for a county and handled many state and federal cases in court, and I learned a lot about civil litigation. My experience doing that helped me invaluably in my divorce practice particularly when it came to high-conflict cases.

The *Family Lawyer Magazine* published an article I wrote, "Utilizing Civil Litigation Techniques in High-Conflict Divorces." It of course was aimed at my fellow lawyers. The main takeaway was that divorce attorneys have an entire playbook available, and a number of the plays in it can help divorce attorneys gain great leverage in certain tough cases. I later did a podcast on the subject but aimed at those actually going through divorce, and here, I offer some of it.

Consider summary judgment motions. These are motions insurance companies or other defense attorneys and civil litigators employ. Such a motion states that there's not enough in a case to warrant going to trial on these issues; it's a request to the judge to throw the whole matter out. Family law attorneys tend not to utilize motions for summary judgment, but when there's a claim of a marital tort—perhaps personal injury caused by a spouse—or if somebody's alleging that against you in instances when you're trying to prove a prenup is not valid or prove that it is, filing a motion for summary judgment can be a very fascinating way to gain some leverage in the litigation to put certain issues to bed and make sure you can focus on the more important issues.

It's not a total victory in family law as it can be in civil litigation because the divorcing parties are still trying to get divorced and address alimony and child-custody issues. One of the standards of summary judgment is that no uncontroverted facts exist and it's really more of a legal argument. You can win on the law on issues of whether a prenup is valid or whether a reconciliation agreement is valid. If you utilize those techniques, you can really go far in gaining leverage and bringing the case to a head.

To that end, another thing that family law attorneys don't do as often as civil litigation attorneys do is depose people. People watching courtroom dramas on TV won't see what went on behind the scenes so to speak—lawyers deposing witnesses way ahead of the trial and simply asking the same questions of the witnesses whether on TV or in reality.

But divorce attorneys can depose witnesses and the other parties thus requiring them to answer questions under oath. Both attorneys will be there, and both can ask questions and cross examine the witnesses and the parties. If their answers change between their deposition and their testimony in court, a lawyer can point that out and cast doubts on their credibility.

In a deposition, a lawyer might ask questions that open up new lines of discovery beyond the actual discovery requests for bank statements, tax returns, and so on. In a high-conflict divorce, depositions could prove to be worth the additional legal costs. Getting someone to admit to something you didn't know in a deposition or having that person contradict what he or she said in a deposition could bring a case back from the brink.

Requests for Admissions are in a way less costly form of a deposition. What they involve is sending other parties a list of questions they have to say yea or nay to. If they don't answer them at all, you can make a motion at trial to essentially state that they have for that reason admitted everything in the statements and therefore waive their right to deny it. You can get a procedural upper hand using Requests for Admissions in that they can give you information that could lead you to uncover useful factual discrepancies.

Another technique that's used a lot in civil litigation but not very much in a New Jersey divorce is a claim of frivolous litigation. Frivolous litigation can occur when people file motion after motion; that can allow you to file a countermotion with the court asking that the person be barred from filing future motions or have to pay for counsel fees.

In many other circumstances, you could claim frivolous litigation if someone falsely claims the other party committed adultery simply to harass that party.

Another element of civil litigation that's not that common in family law is nonspoliation of evidence claims. Usually when a civil litigation case starts out, you'll send a letter to the other side saying in essence, "Please maintain all discovery or potential discovery pertaining to the case. If you don't, it'll be considered a spoliation of evidence." A divorce attorney can tell the other party the same thing, and if the other party pulls embarrassing photos of him or her partying heartily when he or she wants custody of the children and swears he or she is an angel, you can claim that evidence was spoiled. That could lead to an award of damages and positive inferences drawn toward your case. You could also add that as a count in your Complaint for Divorce or counterclaim for divorce; it's another way to gain leverage, and in high-conflict divorces, leverage can play a big role.

When I served as deputy county counsel for Somerset County, the Open Public Records Act (OPRA) I received many, many requests for public records. That gave me a good familiarity with what could be found in public records and how to get that information.

If you have a spouse who works for the government, you might be able to circumvent some of the discovery process by requesting his or her salary or employment information (though some information is exempt from the open-records process). You can end up with information that the opposing party might otherwise object to handing over, and it's another way you can gain leverage by gaining information and move the case forward.

So there you go—a little taste of red meat for those who want to be aggressive in a divorce. But don't say I didn't warn you if the ends don't justify the means. Our firm is in this for the long haul, and we encourage our clients not to burn bridges or take problematic positions and shoot themselves in the foot in the process.

It's sort of like football; you're not going to blitz on every play, but sometimes, an aggressive blitz can disrupt the other side and cause a game-changing turnover. The problem with being aggressive all the time, however, is that you can become easy to read. The element of surprise is important at times in a divorce, and often, litigation boils down to a high-stakes game of chicken.

## DURING THE DIVORCE, SHOULD I LEAVE THE MARITAL HOME?

I get that question a lot, and it's not easy to answer. Let's look at both sides of that question.

### IN FAVOR OF NOT LEAVING THE MARITAL RESIDENCE

The common advice is generally not to leave the marital residence. If you do, you'll have additional expenses, you may hurt your *pendente lite* (during the divorce proceedings) or even post-divorce custody and parenting time (courts may favor the parent with the larger home, one that the children are familiar with and in children's school district), and you may lose some control over the process of listing the property for sale or possession of certain personal items such as furniture. Courts like to favor the *status quo* during the divorce process, and residing together during the divorce helps maintain the *status quo*.

However, a restraining order might force you to leave the house. And if the house is in the other party's name, or if in the prenup you agreed to leave the house in such circumstances, or if for some reason your remaining there wouldn't be in the children's best

**Courts like to favor the *status quo* during the divorce process**

interests, moving out might be best. Again, seek legal help in this matter.

### IN FAVOR OF LEAVING THE MARITAL RESIDENCE

There may be certain variables at play that make it wise for you to leave particularly if your spouse doesn't want to or refuses to leave.

One possible benefit of leaving the marital residence may be achieving peace of mind or at least a break from the turmoil that gets stirred up when both or particularly when just one party wants to divorce.

Although old movies such as *The War of the Roses* may present such issues as farce, it may be difficult to continue to reside with a spouse when there is constant bickering or worse. Also—and this is true particularly for men but could apply to either party—there is some concern that if you do not reside in the marital home, you won't have to worry about your spouse getting an unwarranted restraining order to get you kicked out. Restraining orders are meant to protect people, but they can also be used as weapons to attack people. Law enforcement officers in particular would want to avoid being named in a restraining order; one such incident could stain their records, and they could possibly lose their right to carry a gun.

Divorces can take up to two years if they do not settle, so moving out of the marital residence can help both parties move forward with their lives instead of staying stuck in limbo; that's how clients have told me they've felt when they resided with spouses they were divorcing.

If you decide to vacate the marital residence, take an inventory (on video is best) of all the marital possessions should your spouse later sell or destroy your property or joint legal property. Make copies of *all* important documents you might not be able to copy once you leave.

Leaving the marital residence might raise issues for you if there are children involved as a *pendente lite* order may disfavor you, you may be seen as abandoning the family, and it will be difficult to regain access once you formally vacate. (If you both own the property, there's no legal requirement to leave it unless there's a restraining order or other court order.)

If you decide to vacate the marital residence, take an inventory (on video is best) of all the marital possessions.

Take all these considerations into account whether you decide to stay or leave; a lawyer can be of great help as you sort through all the pros and cons.

## DIVORCE IN THE AGE OF BITCOIN–DIVORCING IN THE TECHNOLOGICAL AGE

Sometimes, I wonder how dogs managed to descended from wolves to the point that they became dogs so domesticated that they can actually enjoy car rides, but I engage in such musings only when I'm really bored.

Divorce lawyers have undergone such evolution over the years as well—they have to constantly adapt to changes not only in the law but also in society at large. When I was in law school, I never thought cryptocurrency could ever be an issue in a divorce case. I didn't even know what it was. But I turned out to be one of the first divorce lawyers in the country to write an article about the need to search for cryptocurrencies in divorce cases.

My attitude toward cryptocurrencies used to be simple—I ignored them and hoped they'd just go away, but divorce lawyers and their clients can no longer bury their heads in the sand. Cryptocurrencies and block-chain technology may or may not be the wave of the future, but they are an increasingly commonly held class of assets that have to be taken into consideration in divorce settlements.

Cryptocurrencies, which I call cryptos, are a form of decentralized virtual currency that were created in 2009 and have been increasingly traded often on virtual currency platforms. They are often owned and traded anonymously and stored in a virtual "wallet," on a smartphone, or in the cloud.

Security is a great concern regarding these types of currencies. Although Bitcoin is the most well-known, there are now various types of this currency, and their value fluctuates so much that they have become the Wild West of speculation. Virtual currencies are an important, cutting-edge topic in some divorces.

Their relative anonymity makes them a difficult asset to locate—meaning they could be a way for someone to hide wealth in a divorce. That means divorce attorneys have to get up to speed on the whole topic.

Lawyers can and should add specific questions about cryptocurrency to all initial discovery and in interrogatories, requests for admissions, at depositions, and at trial—all the way down that road. By specifically asking such questions, the opposing spouse is more likely to be upfront and more likely to be sanctioned if it is later discovered he or she is trying to hide assets in any manner.

Though bitcoins are owned anonymously, their purchase and sale create trails that a forensic expert could discover and a lawyer could subpoena.

Think long and hard about if your spouse could be hiding wealth in this or any other manner such as having some salary stashed in a deferred-compensation account, and talk it over with your lawyer.

# CHAPTER 18

# Paying for Your Divorce

During almost every initial consultation, the biggest elephant in the room is cost. Clients know that getting divorced can be expensive and sometimes prohibitively so. They also know that divorce lawyers generally bill by the hour—hundreds of dollars per. When people say they're concerned about being able to afford a divorce, they have in mind all their regular expenses and perhaps expenses for two households as well as paying child support and alimony.

When I started practicing law, we were in the early stages of the Great Recession. Prior to that, clients could often count on the money they would receive from the sale of their homes to cover their legal bills, but that option dried up as the housing market did.

Unemployment is at or near all-time lows, and the stock and housing markets have rebounded (at the time of this writing), but most Americans do not have $5,000 or more lying around for an initial retainer deposit. Likewise, law firms cannot finance divorced or charge interest on outstanding legal fees. That's why they (and I as well) loathe playing banker, and that can create tension in the relationship and make clients wonder if their lawyers are:

- nickel and diming them to death by charging a lot of nickels and dimes,
- dragging out the case or over-lawyering it,
- working through the retainer quickly and planning on withdrawing from the case if the client cannot replenish it, or
- charging not just for every tiny expense but also for every phone call and email.

These are all legitimate concerns, so attorney and client should discuss what's expected and how the case will be handled. I research studies and surveys about what clients find most dissatisfying about their lawyers, and I then attempt to implement policies that address those concerns or take the opposite tack.

But the cost for a divorce of a modest household may not be all that different from the cost of a divorce of wealthier people; it depends to a big extent on the emotions people bring to a divorce particularly when one party doesn't want to divorce.

Paying for a divorce and particularly the initial retainer is thus sometimes difficult to say the least. I've attempted to make it easy for clients to meet their obligations; for instance, we'll accept payments by **check, cash (with a receipt given), credit card (links for payment through online payment services are given and clients can also pay at the firm's Flemington, New Jersey location) or money order**

As do most lawyers, I expect the retainer amount to be replenished as needed. I encourage clients to call me if they have questions about anything on their bill; I want to know as soon as possible if any client is dissatisfied. Moreover, I attempt not to fully bill for attorney-client communications in divorce matters such as simple calls or emails as I want to keep the lines of communication open as much as possible.

In some cases, I obtain counsel fees from the other party. Nevertheless, I expect payment from my clients, who must then seek reimbursement from their exes. This too is standard in most New Jersey divorce retainer agreements.

A mentor of mine once said it's difficult to make a living as a necessary evil. Few people want to get divorced and pay for the sometimes necessary evil of dueling lawyers who can exacerbate an already difficult situation.

The added benefit of fully understanding the process and your risks, responsibilities, and obligations is the divorce lawyer's stock and trade. If you want to retain my firm but are uncertain if you can afford it, I hope this section will assist you in understanding the potential payment methods and some of the philosophy behind the divorce attorney-client relationship.

## WHO PAYS COUNSEL FEES IN A DIVORCE?

Given the above, you may be concerned about how you'd pay for a divorce attorney particularly if your spouse tries to cut you off from the marital funds. You might need to go to court, but that can be a Catch-22; how can you go to court if you don't have money to pay for the fees the court will want? Likewise, you may be in a marriage in which your spouse earns substantially more than you do or has access to greater assets than you do to pay for lawyers.

New Jersey generally operates under what is known to lawyers as the American system; in essence, it means that each party at court has to pay his or her own legal expenses. Even when what are called "fee-shifting" statutes are involved, it can be difficult to get reimbursed for the costs of litigation. But divorces are different—they generally involve communal money. So who pays?

## WHICH PARTY IS RESPONSIBLE FOR DIVORCE COUNSEL FEES?

The court can make allowance during *pendente lite* (as the divorce is progressing) and on final determination that one party is to pay the other party's legal fees based on the ability of the parties to pay it or part of it, the reasonableness and good faith (or the unreasonableness and bad faith) of the parties, the amount of the fees involved, any fees previously awarded or paid, the results obtained, the degree to which fees were incurred to enforce existing orders or compel discovery, and other factors. The court will also look at the financial circumstances of each party to determine whether counsel fees should be awarded. The court will particularly emphasize any financial disparity between the divorcing parties.

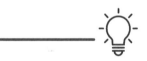

The court will also look at the financial circumstances of each party to determine whether counsel fees should be awarded.

Most counsel fee awards are *without prejudice*, meaning that the court reserves the right to address the final award of counsel fees at the time the divorce is finalized.

If you don't have the funds to seek a divorce but your spouse does, discuss that during an initial consultation with your attorney to determine if appropriate action may be taken to ensure you can afford to keep up with the divorce litigation expenses.

## COLLECTING MONEY DUE IN FAMILY LAW COURT

Marital debt is unlike other types of debt. Most such debt is collected in the Civil Division of the courts particularly the law division (if it's a large debt) or in the Special Civil Part or Small Claims (if less than $15,000). Another interesting fact about collecting money owed to someone in family court matters is that child support may be considered an automatic lien.

Although docketing monies due may still apply in divorce law, there is an easier path to collecting it. This is particularly true in family court cases if a parent owes money and is held in contempt; he or she could be jailed for that until paying up a certain portion of what's due.

Some methods of collection in civil court cases, which may also be pursued as part of enforcement actions in family court matters, include wage garnishment and bank chattel (property) levies. If Probation/Family Support Services is collecting the money, it can act on its own to do so without court intervention.

It's your right to ask that payments be made through the Probation Department, and this is generally chosen over direct pay in New Jersey divorces. Another type of relief that may be pursued is what's known colloquially as a constructive trust— seeking that certain funds (such as retirement funds) be sequestered. That may come in handy if a party owes for college or private education for instance but is not paying. The courts may order that certain funds be liquidated to pay what's due.

## CONSTRUCTIVE TRUSTS

New Jersey law provides in part that:

> If an obligor shall abandon an oblige or separate from the oblige and refuse or neglect to maintain and provide for the oblige, the court may order suitable support and maintenance to be paid and provided by the obligor for the oblige and their children. **If the obligor fails to comply with the order of the court, entered in New Jersey or another jurisdiction, the court may impose a lien against the real and personal property of the obligor who lives in or owns property in New Jersey to secure payment of the overdue support and for such time as the nature of the case and circumstances of the parties render suitable and proper. (emphasis added)**[10]

This means that certain real property can be subject to a lien if the person who has to pay does not do so in a timely fashion.

## LACHES

If you (or your minor children) are owed money, it may be important to act fast to protect your rights in court because courts could impose the doctrine of "laches" against you if you don't pursue your interests. Laches essentially means you slept on your rights. In one case,[11] a party urging application of laches must demonstrate that the other party delayed in asserting a claim now stale without explanation or excuse, that the delay was unreasonable given the circumstances, and that the delay was prejudicial to the party urging the defense.

---

10    N.J.S.A. 2A:34-23.

11    *Rolnick v. Rolnick*, 262 N.J. Super. 343 (App. Div. 1993).

Collecting money due to you in a New Jersey divorce action can be tedious and make you feel you're throwing good money after bad. Indeed, a large percentage of child support and alimony ordered or agreed to is never paid. I've been able to utilize creative methods throughout my career to assist clients in getting what they and their children are due, but these matters have to undergo a strict cost-benefit analysis; spending $500 to collect $100 just doesn't make sense.

## IF ONE OF US REMARRIES, DOES THAT AFFECT CHILD SUPPORT?

If your ex recently remarried or is about to have children in a later relationship, you might be concerned about how this could affect your own children's child support. I will limit this discussion to situations in which an ex is recently remarried or is recently a new parent from a later relationship.

In one important case,[12] the New Jersey supreme court acknowledged the right of trial courts to modify support provisions at any time provided there is a "permanent and substantial change in circumstances." The court gave examples of such changed circumstances including these.

- an increase in the cost of living
- an increase or decrease in the supporting spouse's income
- a party's illness, disability, or infirmity arising after the original judgment
- the dependent spouse's loss of a house or apartment
- the dependent spouse's cohabitation with another

---

12   *Lepis v. Lepis*, 83 N.J. 139 (1980).

- subsequent employment by the dependent spouse
- changes in federal income tax law

This of course assumes that the circumstances have indeed changed and the party can show that.

Another important case[13] stated that in high-income child-support cases, a balance must be struck between reasonable needs that reflect lifestyle opportunities while precluding an inappropriate windfall to children or infringing on the legitimate right of either parent to determine the appropriate lifestyle of the children.

In another important case,[14] the court said, "The custodial parent should not gain a benefit through the guise of child support that is beyond that which is more than incidental to the benefits being conferred to the child."

*Strahan v. Strahan* developed that concept further and reminded courts that it was important in high-income cases that judges analyze the reasonableness of the needs claimed by the custodial parent of the children.

One law[15] specifically provides that child-support guidelines can be modified or disregarded by the court only where good cause is shown. Child-support guidelines say that if the net income of the parties is greater than $187,200 per year, the court must apply child-support guidelines up to $187,200 and thereafter may but is not required to supplement additional income based on certain factors.

---

13  *Isaacson v. Isaacson.*
14  *Loro v. Del Colliano.*
15  R. 5:6A.

The law says that in deciding a child-support amount, the court should consider the following factors.

- the needs of the child
- the standard of living and economic circumstances of each parent
- all sources of income and assets of each parent
- the earning ability of the parents including their educational backgrounds
- all sources of income and assets of each parent
- the need and capacity of the child for education
- the age and health of the child and the parents
- income, assets, and earning ability of the child
- responsibility of the parents for court-ordered support of others
- reasonable debts and liabilities of child and each parent
- any other factor the court deems relevant

The above provides a framework of child-support modification in New Jersey (upward or downward). Although your ex might have a better standard of living after remarrying or cohabitating the new spouse or partner doesn't have any obligation to provide support for your children. That means the court will not impute additional income to your ex or consider his or her new spouse's income requiring a recalculation of child support. If a child is born from a subsequent marriage or relationship, however, then courts may consider that to be an appropriate permanent and substantial change in circumstances warranting a recalculation of child support.

The guidelines take into consideration how subsequent children may impact child support. In that situation, you may be entitled to learn about the new spouse's or partner's finances to determine just how much support your ex is diverting to a child from his or her new relationship.

These matters tend to be very fact-sensitive and can get complicated. If you have any questions regarding modifying child support after your ex remarries or cohabitates, consult with a New Jersey divorce lawyer.

Remember that the same would apply to you if the situations were reversed.

## CHAPTER 19

# *Types of Experts Available for a Contested New Jersey Divorce*

**Unfortunately,** not every family law matter is simple. Particularly in contested divorces or other contested family law matters, a need may arise for one or more experts. This chapter will briefly review some of the more common types of experts. These experts will often review materials, meet with parties and their children, write reports, and sometimes testify in court. Some experts are ordered by the court and others are retained by the parties. In addition, each party may retain their own experts or agree upon a joint expert.

## REAL ESTATE APPRAISERS

If there is a question about the value of a marital home or other real estate, a real estate agent may be retained to perform a real estate appraisal including what repairs might need to be made to make a house marketable. This can be particularly necessary when the parties cannot agree to repairs, a listing date, or a sales price.

## FORENSIC ACCOUNTANTS

A common concern among parties is that one or the other might be hiding assets. The discovery process can address this, but sometimes, it requires a forensic accountant to follow the trail of money and assets.

## CHILD-CUSTODY EXPERTS

Certain psychologists specialize in meeting with the children and the parents and advising them on the best custody and parenting-time schedules.

## APPRAISERS

When someone has a rare stamp or sports memorabilia collection, sometimes an expert in a specific field might be required to appraise the value of those items.

## BUSINESS APPRAISERS

The valuation of a business can at times be the most important issue to resolve in a divorce. One or both parties may be the owners of a closely held business or corporation. After an analysis is conducted to determine whether the business is subject to equitable distribution, the major issue becomes one of valuation, and that can get complicated, but it nonetheless would be nearly impossible to settle a divorce without agreement on this important issue.

Often, experts will be retained to evaluate a business. It could be that someone is a partner in a business but doesn't have that much control over it, and that could affect how much his or share of it is worth as opposed to someone who has total control over a business.

Keep in mind that businesses may appear less profitable than usual because from 2017 to 2022, the 50 percent cap on business expenses will be replaced by a business's ability to fully deduct certain business expenses such as for new computers. Accordingly, it may appear on paper that businesses were less profitable and there is perhaps greater room for gamesmanship in this area.

## EMPLOYMENT/EMPLOYABILITY EXPERTS

If someone is suspected of purposefully being unemployed or underemployed, an employment expert might be retained to review the individual's work history and degrees and draft a report about his or her income-earning potential.

The above are just some of the many potential experts that may be retained in certain New Jersey family law actions.

# CHAPTER 20

# Assets Not Subject to Equitable Distribution

**In general,** most property owned by a divorcing couple in New Jersey is subject to equitable distribution, but certain assets are normally excluded from equitable distribution in New Jersey. Please note that for all of the following, there is no bright-line rule. If someone inherits a chunk of money and puts it into a joint IRA, that could be considered commingling funds and thus making them marital assets.

## PREMARITAL PROPERTY

Equitable distribution traditionally refers to property that's acquired *during* a marriage. If you enter into a marriage with a house, for example, that house will likely not be subject to equitable distribution if you divorce. Again, this is a fact-sensitive determination; you have to speak with an attorney or other expert to determine if it's in fact excluded from equitable distribution.

If property is commingled—for instance, if a spouse's name is later included on the deed or if a spouse has contributed a whole bunch of sweat equity to upgrading his or her spouse's inherited house—that spouse might be able to stake a claim that it has become marital property.

There are numerous caveats to the following examples, but I offer them here just to let readers know some of the concerns they should be aware of.

## GIFTS AND INHERITANCES

Gifts and inheritances from third parties are often not subject to equitable distribution. Gifts the divorcing parties gave to each other during the marriage, however, (think jewelry or cars here) will likely be considered marital assets and thus subject to equitable distribution.

**Gifts and inheritances from third parties are often not subject to equitable distribution.**

Gifts that others have given to both spouses are likely subject to equitable distribution. Some in-laws might give a car, say, to a couple but later claim it was meant solely for their son or daughter. The burden of proof generally falls on the party seeking the exception.

## PERSONAL-INJURY SETTLEMENTS

The portion of a personal-injury settlement awarded for physical or emotional pain is generally not subject to equitable distribution, but the rest of that settlement (say to repair a jointly owned SUV) can be considered marital property.

Even when one party is the breadwinner and the other party does not work outside the home, unless there's an exception such as outlined above, most property will be subject to

equitable distribution. But keep in mind that the above exceptions are very fact sensitive, so speak with an attorney licensed
in your area and who practices in this area of law.

## LIFE INSURANCE OBLIGATIONS

Not too many people find insurance all that interesting. Most
of us consider it something we need but not something we like
to think about. Accidental death. Life insurance. Health insurance. These are insurance policies that seem to only pay out
when something bad has happened.

But insurance can play an important role in a New Jersey
Divorce, in particular, life insurance whether term or whole life.

Term life insurance is less expensive and contains merely a
death benefit; it has no value other than when the person with
the policy dies, so it will not factor into equitable distribution

Whole life insurance may have a value aside from its death
benefit; the person holding the policy might build up equity in
it over the years, and thus it will need to be accounted for when
it comes to equitable distribution.

## LIFE INSURANCE DURING THE DIVORCE PROCESS

New Jersey laws require that each party maintains the status
quo of the marriage as the divorce is progressing, and that
means keeping up payments on insurance policies of all types.
If, say, the wife always paid for term insurance naming the children as beneficiaries, she must continue to do so throughout the
divorce process. The parties must also provide the court with
insurance information after a divorce complaint is filed.

## LIFE INSURANCE DURING DIVORCE NEGOTIATIONS

Life insurance will factor heavily in two sections of the Marital Settlement Agreement that cover equitable distribution and the requirement that life insurance premiums be paid. This is because a life insurance policy will make sure alimony, child support, and contributions to college educations will continue if the payor dies.

## ALIMONY DEDUCTION ELIMINATED

The most well-known impact of the reform is that commencing January 1, 2019 you can no longer deduct alimony payments on your taxes and alimony received will not be considered income. This portion of the act eliminated a seventy-five-year-old tax provision and has been referred to by some as a divorce penalty.

# CHAPTER 21

## *Dissipating Funds during the Divorce*

One of the basic tenants of a New Jersey divorce is that unless both parties agree or the court approves of it, neither party can dissipate marital assets during a divorce. This makes a lot of sense; all the money has to be accounted for and divided fairly. Nonetheless, people have tried to dissipate assets in their favor, and at times, it can take a forensic accountant to uncover that. Here are some ways marital assets can be dissipated

1. encumbering a marital asset with a loan (say a line of credit on a home)
2. spending cash in joint bank accounts
3. selling an asset such as a car without permission of the court or the other party
4. giving marital property away
5. changing or even trying to change property titles to one name
6. allowing loans to go into default
7. allowing a family business to decline in value

As you can imagine, there are many other instances where the alienation, encumbering, dissipation, and so on of marital assets can occur. Although the definition of "dissipation" is somewhat nebulous, in cases where it can be demonstrated, it can lead to the one doing the dissipating having to pay counsel fees and pay back the amounts dissipated or other sanctions. In one case,[16] a court ruled that someone who had gambled away a lot of money had to reimburse the other party.

The court could require party accused of dissipating assets to prove that it was a legitimate move or that the asset was not a marital asset such as gifts, inheritances, and assets that preceded the marriage and thus aren't subject to equitable distribution.

Often during the *pendente lite* phase of litigation, a party will request nondissipation as part of a motion. One party can file an Order to Show Cause (or a motion if time is not a big issue right then) seeking that the party stop dissipating marital assets. Large-scale dissipation is not as common as one might expect, but this issue often rears its head at some point on a small scale in almost every case. For instance, a client might ask his or her attorney, "Can I sell some of these old books on eBay?" But if those books are considered joint marital assets, even such an innocent action might draw the ire of the other party. Clients and their lawyers have to keep this in mind as a divorce is proceeding.

---

16   *Siegel v. Siegel* (1990).

# CHAPTER 22

# *Family Law Appeals*

Given the nature of family law cases, parties are often unsatisfied with the decision made at the trial court level and want to appeal a decision. But family law appeals are rare for several reasons. First, they are very expensive. The party filing the appeal has to obtain the transcripts from the trial court, and that can cost a lot. Also, filing an appeal is a labor-intensive process, thus legal costs will be high. Second, because case law tells the appellate court to give lower court judges a great deal of latitude in their decisions, appeals will often be unsuccessful. Third, parties don't get a lot of time to decide to appeal a ruling.

> Appeals from final judgments of courts, final judgment or orders of judges sitting as statutory agents and final judgments of the Division of Workers' Compensation shall be taken within 45 days of their entry. However, appeals from final judgments terminating parental rights shall be taken within 21 days of their entry.[17]

Moreover, if the matter is appealed, the appellate court decision could be appealed to the New Jersey supreme court, and that

---

17    This is the relevant part of R. 2:4-1(a).

means cases could be tied up for years. That may be fine for major corporations or governmental agencies, but family law involves individuals. It is more common, for even a successful appeal to lead to a "remand" whereby the case is sent back to the original trial court for additional rulings. For many, the appeals process simply demands too much and offers too little.

That said, every case is different and entirely fact-sensitive. At times, I've advised my clients to appeal, and at other times, I've given some the pros and cons of their particular appeals and they decided not to appeal. A point to keep in mind is that any appeal court will not look at any new evidence, just what was presented to the lower court.

Although appeals are rare, they are an important part of our state's judicial process. At times and under the right set of facts or circumstances, our appellate courts even rise beyond the function of correcting a mistake to the level of righting a wrong or even creating new law or a different interpretation of the law.

An appeal
court will not
look at any new
evidence.

# CHAPTER 23

## *What If I'm Not Happy with My Divorce Lawyer?*

I have a friend from another jurisdiction who has called me a few times about a divorce. I told this friend I couldn't provide legal advice because it was a different jurisdiction and the friend was represented by counsel. She asked if I would simply listen to her situation; she wanted to know whether she should change divorce lawyers. From her perspective, her lawyer was

- slow to respond or communicate,
- dismissive of her ideas,
- sent bills that were difficult to understand and seemed really high,
- failed to push the case forward and seemed to be dragging it out, and
- did not educate her about her rights and responsibilities or his game plan moving forward.

I asked her if she had mentioned any of this to her attorney, and the answer was no. She'd dutifully loaded up her retainer as had been agreed to for perhaps a year but hadn't complained about any of this. Lawyers have a general ethical requirement to communicate with their clients, but retainer language aside, there's no requirement that their clients communicate with them.

This was a great lesson for me because I was able to see a divorce through a client's perspective without any prior history or my own opinions or emotions being involved. I knew this was logical and hardworking and not tough to get along with. I have had clients advise me they were not satisfied with the process and at times not happy with some of my advice (sometimes emphatically so), but I could always brush it off as the clients being the type who wouldn't be satisfied with a reincarnated Clarence Darrow representing them. Or so my ego likes to believe.

How can lawyers effectively communicate with their clients who are quietly unhappy? Since I've opened my firm, I've always given my clients my cell phone, and I attempt to answer their calls even on weekends, at night, and sometimes during holidays. I've learned that that's not always sufficient because some people don't like conflict.

Regardless, I really want to know when my clients are unhappy with me, our staff, the direction of the case, or our firm in general. A bad slice of pizza is a couple of bucks down the drain, but a bad relationship with a lawyer that ends up with a Divorce Agreement someone's not happy with will cost a whole lot more in terms of time, angst, and money. I never want that to be the case with my clients.

That means at times I have to point out to my clients that they're not likely to get the other party or the courts to go along with this or that desire they have and it would be wasted money to file certain motions. I always want them to bring to my attention anything they don't understand about their cases so I can fill them in with developments whether they're good or bad news.

Lawyers should regularly follow up with their clients to ensure they know the process and that they're happy with or at least understand what progress has been made in their cases. At times, my clients have challenged me and pointed out things in agreements that changed my thinking. It's really a team effort particularly in these days when clients are more sophisticated than ever thanks to technology and the internet.

Lawyers and clients should not be afraid to walk away from each other if a case isn't a good fit, and I've done that. A solid initial consultation will hopefully allow clients and lawyers alike a good opportunity to make the decision to team up or part ways—no hard feelings.

As the experts, lawyers should provide their clients with resources so they can understand the flow of a divorce, and they should never sugarcoat the process or the likely results. This saves clients time and money and helps make discussions between attorney and client more productive. I'd much rather have clients who seek resources through my website rather than on the internet at large because I know what I have to offer in that regard, and I know it applies to New Jersey law, a critical point.

Enough dancing around the issue. Should a client change lawyers in the middle of a divorce? The answer is nuanced; nobody but the client can decide that. Changing divorce lawyers in New Jersey may require certain court procedures such as entry of a substitution of attorney. And when you hire a new lawyer in the middle of a divorce, you'll likely have to pay money (and sometimes a lot) for your new lawyer to read all the pleadings, correspondence, and other documents to get up to speed with your particular case.

Some attorneys see a prospective client with multiple attorneys as a potential red flag, and some attorneys' policy is never to accept cases they did not start.

But beware of the sunk-cost fallacy: a bad bargain or bad relationship may not improve in time (things generally tend to get worse), and staying in a bad attorney-client situation just because you already paid a lot of money may not improve your situation.

You get only one shot at a divorce. You can often modify terms after a divorce, but if you're dissatisfied, it's best to take action before the trial or before signing off on a binding agreement.

Be honest about the situation: is your lawyer really incompetent or acting inappropriately, or are you merely upset about the case in general? Even with a great divorce lawyer, the results may not be all you had hoped for, the case might take longer than expected, and it may cost more than you expected to spend. There are many factors at play in a divorce, some of which are out of our control. Consider therapy to help you deal with the stress of a long, drawn-out divorce.

Does your lawyer communicate with you on a regular basis? Does the lawyer quickly return you calls? Explain your invoices if asked? Answer your questions? Seem to know what he or she is talking about? Those are the baseline requirements and may even be ethical imperatives. If these questions are not in the affirmative, it may be worth considering new counsel.

## CONCLUSION

Only you can determine whether an attorney-client privilege is worth continuing. I hope the above assists you in considering the unique nature of a New Jersey divorce lawyer/client relationship. I have changed doctors and other professionals often without telling them why. A good lawyer will want to hear your concerns and have the opportunity to earn your continued business. That said, in some instances, a fresh start may be necessary and appropriate.

## CHAPTER 24

# Equitable Distribution of Personal-Injury Employment Discrimination and Workers' Compensation Awards in New Jersey

**If you or your spouse** has received or will receive a payout for personal injury, workers' comp claim, or employment discrimination, that will affect in divorces and even prenups.

A personal-injury award such as one from an auto accident or a slip and fall can at times get up into the hundreds of thousands. The general idea in the law[18] is that any such money meant to repair or replace a car is considered a marital asset, but money meant to compensate a victim for pain and suffering or mental and physical disabilities isn't (that is, unless it is deliberately comingled with marital assets).

Likewise, the amount awarded to the noninjured spouse for "lack of consortium"—in the case that an injured spouse can no longer perform sexually to the detriment of his or her spouse as well—stays with that uninjured spouse and is not considered

---

18  *Landwehr v. Landwehr*, 111 N.J. 491, 495 (1988).

a marital asset. Any portion of a settlement compensating for lost earnings, medical expenses, or the like are subject to equitable distribution.

The idea here is that any amount meant to cover lost wages and expenses, which are marital in nature, are to be distributed. The courts say that someone claiming an asset is not marital property has to demonstrate that.

There are other important details in these matters. The part of an award meant to compensate an injured person for a permanent disability that reduces his or her earnings potential is not ordinarily considered a marital asset. (I use the word "ordinarily" here to underscore the fact that the law can be complex and is always fact-sensitive.)

Similarly, the portion of a disability pension representing the retirement portion is subject to equitable distribution, whereas any income compensation or reimbursement for personal loss from the disability would not be subject to equitable distribution, but that can be difficult to establish.

In medical malpractice and employment-discrimination awards, the same principles apply—how much was meant to compensate the harmed individual specifically, and how much was meant to compensate both husband and wife? And what happens if a lawsuit is pending while a couple are in the process of divorcing? One court ruling said that the parties had to decide how to split that money up (assuming they received it) after they divorce.

> Money meant to compensate a victim for pain and suffering or mental and physical disabilities is no a marital asset.

In terms of punitive damages that can be awarded in a personal-injury case, no New Jersey case law covers how they should be divided if at all, but rulings outside New Jersey might establish a precedent for New Jersey courts in certain cases. As a practical matter, it would be rare to come across a divorce case in which distribution or division of punitive damages would be an issue, but it could happen.

Because pain and suffering claims are generally not taxable (but awards for lost wages generally are subject to taxation), there's an inherent incentive in personal-injury actions for the injured individual to seek lump-sum pain and suffering pay-outs, but that could cloud a fair distribution of marital assets in a divorce.

If you have a matter involving pending awards, your divorce attorney might want to speak with your personal-injury attorney to determine how the settlement might be structured. The two can work together to determine the best course of action—maybe taking depositions, crafting the discovery process, and so on to make sure these issues are ultimately nailed down.

Though family law attorneys and personal-injury attorneys often attempt to avoid any overlap between proceedings, that could occur, and it could even warrant calling in an estate attorney to develop a more holistic approach to these types of issues.

As is the case with most of family law, distribution of funds from worker's compensation, personal injury, and the like is extremely fact-sensitive. Accordingly, it may be important to meet with an attorney to determine how your specific facts may be applied particularly in a post-alimony reform world in New Jersey.

## CHAPTER 25

# An Overview of Domestic-Violence Law in New Jersey

**This is merely a brief overview** of New Jersey domestic-violence law; whole books have been written on this important subject itself. But in essence, the 1991 Prevention of Domestic Violence Act was a response to the New Jersey legislature's findings that domestic violence was "a serious crime against society with a large number of victims that were not receiving proper protection under the present laws."

## CONFIDENTIALITY AND RESTRAINING ORDERS

The act itself requires confidential statistical record-keeping, but the test for confidentiality is performed on a case-by-case basis balancing the potential harm to the victim, possible discouragement of the victim coming forward, and the balance of First-Amendment confidentiality interests.

## DEFINITION OF "VICTIM" UNDER THE ACT

1.  any person who is eighteen or older
2.  an emancipated minor who has been subjected to domestic violence by a spouse, former spouse, or any other person who is a present or former household member
3.  any person regardless of age with whom the victim has a child in common or with whom the victim anticipates having a child in common if one of the parties is pregnant
4.  any person who has been subjected to domestic violence by a person with whom the victim has had a dating relationship (but this cannot be applied retroactively).

## THE BATTERED-SPOUSE DEFENSE

This is a defense created in a murder case[19] by which a battered spouse may argue a form of self-defense even if a murder was committed during a time when the victim's life was not immediately in danger, for instance, when a spouse is sleeping. The victim must argue that she (or he) was certain that if she didn't kill her spouse, she would be killed due to a long history of domestic violence. The case held that battered-woman's syndrome was relevant to the honesty and reasonableness of the defendant's belief that she was in imminent danger of death or serious injury and was an appropriate subject for expert testimony (a very rare and somewhat controversial clause).

## TEMPORARY RESTRAINING ORDERS (TROS)

---

19   *State v. Kelly,* (Supreme Court of NJ, 1984).

There is now a two-part system whereby a victim can seek a temporary restraining order (TRO) and then a final restraining order (FRO). In New Jersey, an FRO extends indefinitely unless extinguished by a judge after a formal hearing.

The three factors for the issuance of a TRO are these.

1.  Does the plaintiff qualify as a victim? (see above)
2.  Did the defendant commit an act of domestic violence?
3.  Is there a history of domestic violence?

The types of relief that may be available under a TRO include injunctions barring the defendant from returning to the scene, possessing firearms (as mentioned, this is so important for law enforcement personnel), having no contact with the victim, granting victim exclusive use and occupancy of the residence, granting temporary custody of any child in common to the victim, and providing for interim parenting time for defendant granting temporary financial support.

A victim seeking a TRO has to give sworn testimony in court or via electronic communication. If the court refuses to issue a TRO, the victim can still seek and receive an emergency *ex parte* hearing *de novo*—a new hearing—from the Family Part of the proper county superior court. The defendant may also have a right to return to the scene while supervised (almost always by police officers) to retrieve personal belongings.

## THE DOMESTIC-VIOLENCE COMPLAINT

The complaint must be filed through the superior court, Family Part, or on an emergency basis through a superior or municipal court judge. Each complaint must allege at least one cause of action for domestic violence. Generally, a confidential Victim Information Sheet is also required to be filled out at the time the complaint is filed.

## DISCOVERY AT A FINAL RESTRAINING ORDER HEARING

Discovery at these hearings is only with court approval after a showing of good cause. This is why some attorneys refer to domestic-violence trials as the Wild West or Trial by Ambush. There are generally no depositions or formal discovery actions. Discovery items you may wish to procure include relevant police reports, TRO transcripts, complaints, 911 transcripts, pertinent medical records, and potential subpoenas for any out-of-court witnesses.

## STANDARD OF REVIEW/STANDARD OF PROOF

The standards for TROs (and FROs) is proof by the preponderance of the evidence. For related criminal charges such as contempt, the standard is beyond a reasonable doubt.

## FINAL RESTRAINING ORDERS

Getting an FRO requires satisfactory answers to these questions.

1. Does the plaintiff qualify as a victim under the act?
2. Did the defendant commit an act of domestic violence?
3. Is there a history of domestic violence?
4. Was the domestic violence particularly harmful?

The fourteen domestic-violence offenses recognized by New Jersey are the following.

1. homicide
2. assault
3. terroristic threats
4. kidnapping
5. criminal restraint
6. false imprisonment
7. sexual assault
8. criminal sexual contact
9. lewdness
10. criminal mischief
11. burglary
12. criminal trespass
13. harassment
14. stalking

The most common elements I see in my practice are allegations of harassment with assault coming in second. Definitions for harassment are the same as criminal harassment (domestic-violence actions being considered *quasi*-criminal). A touchstone of harassment is demonstrating a purpose of intent to harass on the part of the defendant. If there is a history of violence, an incident that could be considered ambiguous could result in an FRO being issued. If not, an "egregious" action is required. A history of domestic violence need not be proven by prior adjudications.

## *APPEALS OF FINAL RESTRAINING ORDERS*

Findings are binding on appeal when supported by adequate credible evidence. Great deference is thus generally given to the trial court judge's determination given that such evidence is largely testimonial. Family court judges' expertise in such matters is thus noted.

## TYPES OF RELIEF OFFERED BY A RESTRAINING ORDER

1. economic relief (temporary transfer of real/personal property, damages, support—but not equitable distribution)
2. custody/parenting-time modification
3. all other relief appropriate to prevent further abuse
4. barring future acts of domestic violence
5. barring certain locations (home and work)
6. barring contacting the victim
7. barring entering a certain proximity near the victim
8. modifying drop-off/pick-up schedule for parenting time
9. barring weapons and issuing a search warrant for weapons
10. ordering counseling
11. vacating the marital residence

## MARITAL TORTS (TEVIS CLAIMS)

Domestic violence may be utilized in a divorce lawsuit for seeking specific damages known as Tevis Claims; they are akin to personal-injury claims in civil litigation.

## DISMISSAL OF RESTRAINING ORDERS

FROs are permanent unless dismissed by a court. A court could do that based on a number of factors including these.

1. victim's consent
2. victim's fear of defendant
3. current relationship between the parties
4. number of contempt convictions if any
5. defendant's use of drugs and alcohol
6. defendant's violence toward others
7. counseling
8. age and health of defendant
9. whether plaintiff is acting in good faith in opposing the dismissal
10. whether another jurisdiction has an order protecting the victim from the defendant
11. any other relevant reason a restraining order should be dismissed.

A defendant moving for dismissal must also demonstrate the lapse of a year, good cause, and a substantial change in circumstances considered with the history. If the plaintiff moves, good cause need not be shown, but the plaintiff must demonstrate that the request was made voluntarily and without coercion.

Conversely, contempt of a restraining order (whether a TRO or a FRO) could be considered a fourth-degree crime.

## CIVIL RESTRAINTS

Domestic-violence matters cannot be negotiated under the law, but courts may allow "civil restraints" to be entered into between the parties. Such an order would have a no-contact provision but would lack the teeth of a formal restraining order should the defendant violate it. Civil restraints cannot be entered into on the domestic-violence docket but rather during a concurrent proceeding such as a divorce or legal separation action.

My experience serving as the appointed municipal prosecutor in various towns has taught me firsthand that it is difficult for victims to push forward with charges in a criminal setting as well as in family court. Make sure you take the appropriate steps to be safe if this portion of the book pertains to you or someone you know.

# CHAPTER 26

# Happily *Even* After

**We're finally there:** the *Paradiso* section of this book. We've covered the basics of New Jersey divorce law and have an idea of how to navigate it to our advantage and maintain focus on our long-term goals—to end up with a fair divorce and a solid chance at a brighter future.

This chapter includes advice on how to script your post-divorce life to make sure you can move forward to greener pastures and avoid common land mines after your divorce.

This is the goal, the nirvana, the end game. If you're going through a divorce or already divorced, this chapter can help you visualize what your Happily *Even* After can look like.

## WHAT IS HAPPILY *EVEN* AFTER?

Many people give up on marriage too easily. I see it all the time in my practice. Others tend to hang on too long to bad marriages due to inertia caused by their particular situations. They let emotions such as a fear of change get in the way of their happiness. Many people equate divorce and death, but divorce can offer a chance of rebirth. Like a phoenix, you can rise from the ashes of your failed marriage and become who you were meant to be. Your children can be happy and you too if you handle your divorce and its aftermath to the best of your abilities.

When we were kids, we read fairy tales about people meeting the right people and living happily ever after. Living Happily *Even* After is the living embodiment of the idea that your best days are ahead and that though you have a long and arduous journey ahead of you if you decide to divorce, you can get through the circles of hell and to your *paradiso* whatever that may be. Part of that may involve new activities, new friends, new loved ones, and new thought processes.

## LOOSE BAGGAGE: COMMON POST-DIVORCE ISSUES

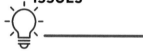

Like a phoenix, you can rise from the ashes of your failed marriage and become who you were meant to be.

When individuals finally get divorced, in many instances, they've reached the end of a long journey. Like Dante, they have gone through hell and purgatory in order to hopefully reach heaven. The hell of divorce is the uncertainty, the breakdown of a sacred trust that will affect everything from finances to the time one gets to spend with their children. The purgatory in my (admittedly extended) metaphor is the waiting—waiting to finalize an agreement, waiting for court dates for a trial, waiting with no certainty as to the outcome. The type of heaven offered is merely this: the chance to pick up the pieces and move forward with your life.

Unfortunately, the finalization of a divorce does not often absolve one of dealing with an ex. Besides issues of coparenting or finalizing the sale of property, there may also be retirement accounts to be divided and a myriad of other loose ends to tie up. You should make plans to change your will and the beneficiaries of your life insurance and so on if you have not already done so.

Marital Settlement Agreements are sometimes not the panacea people hoped for. I advise my clients that the MSA is essentially a rulebook. It advises the parties of their rights and responsibilities in their new post-divorce lives including who can claim the children on their taxes or who gets the children on which Thanksgiving or Christmas, but it cannot address every issue that might arise post-divorce. Nor can it except with court intervention force the other party to comply with its language. It is the goal of most divorces and perhaps the most important document in family law, but it is neither all-encompassing nor intractable no matter how well drafted.

As I mentioned before, a post-divorce change in circumstances may warrant modifying the MSA. The Great Recession, for instance, drove down house values drastically, and that constituted a changed circumstance that warranted a reduction in child support or alimony. None of us can guess the future and know for sure that an MSA will answer all eventualities in the next five, ten, or twenty years.

There are certain motions that exes can make after a divorce, and here are some.

1. **Motion to Enforce Litigant's Rights**—filed when one party is not complying with the terms of the divorce or subsequent court orders

2. **Motion to Modify Alimony or Child Support**—Is there a "permanent and substantial" change in circumstances warranting the modification of alimony or child support upward or downward?

3. **Motion to Emancipate Children**—New Jersey uses a nebulous standard ("Has the child moved beyond the sphere and influence of his or her parents?") to determine emancipation. Absent consent of the parties, this issue often needs to be proven in court via a motion.

4. **Motion to Relocate**—In New Jersey, the custodial parent generally needs the consent of the other party or the court's permission to relocate to a different state.

5. **Motion to Modify Parenting Time or Custody**—Was there a change warranting a modification of previously ordered or agreed-to custody or parenting time?

And so on specific to the facts of each case.

In short, when your divorce is finalized and the bittersweet moment comes that you are no longer legally married, remember that there might be additional issues in the future. Enjoy the moment, but keep your records organized, and make sure that you and your ex comply with the terms of your MSA. The more the parties can work together (absent domestic-violence issues, etc.), the more they'll be able to avoid more legal fees post-divorce. By preparing for these loose ends, your post-divorce life will not be derailed before you get a chance to move forward.

## THE BENEFITS OF WORKING WITH YOUR SPOUSE POST-DIVORCE

Just because two people are divorced doesn't mean they'll cease having a relationship of some kind. They'll often still have to work together with regards to their children and other issues. Sometimes, parties are able to work together in the best interests of their children, but at other times, old wounds can reopen and make it difficult to agree or compromise.

### HOLIDAY PARENTING TIME

Let's say the father is supposed to exercise parenting time on the Fourth of July, but he's called in to work that day at the last minute. If the parties get along, he might be able to call the mother and work out an arrangement that is mutually beneficial for all.

On the other hand, if the parties get worked up over this issue, they might have to call in their attorneys and pay perhaps thousands to work out certain issues that shouldn't have been contentious.

### FINANCIALS

I've also seen instances in which where one party loses a job and both parties compromise on alimony until he or she finds a new job instead of filing a costly motion for post-judgment relief. The point is that there will likely be times when each party needs the assistance of the other whether they like it or not. In those instances, the warm memory of a previous accommodation might be remembered.

## AVOIDING OUTSIDE INTERVENTION

**In some instances,** court, attorney, or other intervention is required, say, when one party is not being reasonable or a child's safety or health might be at risk. But there are also other times when the parties could probably work something out. That's the best option for ensuring smooth sailing post-divorce.

## CUSTODY OF PETS

Divorcing couples can disagree when it comes to custody of pets. I'm a dog person, so here, I'll focus on dogs mainly because I don't want to risk upsetting my collie Isla by choosing cats over dogs in this hypothetical analysis. Unlike Lassie, she would find a way to get even!

Dogs don't become issues in divorces as much as some nondivorce attorneys might think, but there have been cases in which people have spent years and perhaps hundreds of thousands of dollars fighting over a beloved family dog. Those of course are the exception to the rule, but the custody of a dog can become a bone of contention.

The custody of dogs are usually worked out amicably and included in the Marital Settlement Agreement, but keep in mind that this is an area of law that is in flux. I can't guarantee the veracity of this story, but I heard from a good source that a judge once told a divorcing couple who were arguing over custody of their dog, "Both parties need to agree to an arrangement for the dog within forty-eight hours or I'll rule that the dog be sent to the SPCA."

Such modern-day King Solomon rulings are becoming increasingly rarer as pets are more often being seen as a part of the family rather than merely property—something us pet owners have known all along.. Though dogs are getting more respect in New Jersey courtrooms, they are still currently seen only as an elevated form of property on par with family heirlooms for example.

A divorcing couple has some options to keep a judge from having to rule on this issue. An MSA might read, "Husband gets Fido whenever he has parenting time with the kids" or "Wife gets Spot one month, Husband gets Spot the next."

If the divorcing couple cannot agree to give custody of a dog to one or the other or share the dog, the courts will want to know if the dog belonged to one or the other prior to the marriage, if there are children who are attached to the dog, who's better able to care for it, and so on.

I always urge my clients to work out some agreement on dog matters with their soon-to-be exes; that's so much better than spending money litigating the issue and having a judge decide the matter for them.

## WHAT CAN WE LEARN ABOUT PERSONAL FINANCE FROM DIVORCED COUPLES?

A little-known fact about me is that up until about ten years ago, I used to blog about personal finance. My website eventually received thousands of unique visitors per month and actually generated some money that helped me pay down some of my then-significant student loans. I sold the blog because I wanted to focus solely on my clients, and about eight years after I graduated from law school and my wife received a master's in school psychology, she and I had paid off close to $200,000 in student loans. Other than our mortgage, we're debt free.

Personal finance has always interested me—leaning ways to pay off loans efficiently, in what to invest, how to save, and how to handle taxes. That background and interest has assisted me a lot in my law practice because a great deal of family law involves family and personal finances. I often jokingly refer to divorce law as personal finance with someone you now hate.

The Case Information Statement (CIS) that the court requires each divorcing spouse to fill out has a Schedule C, essentially a monthly budget that goes down the line to even expenses for toiletries. You're also required to list all your assets and liabilities to help determine a net worth. Statistics and math come into play in negotiating the division of retirement accounts, stock options, IRAs, and the like.

Many people find that boring, but it's right up my alley. Even better, I have learned a great deal about personal finance from going through numerous divorces with my clients. There are many takeaways that can assist all of us—even those not currently contemplating divorce. Here are some of the takeaways I have learned from clients' divorces that might help you during your divorce or post-divorce.

## BE AWARE OF YOUR FAMILY'S FINANCES

Though one spouse may take the lead in handling personal finances, it's important that both of them understand their family's complete financial picture. This is important for a number of reasons not the least of which is that financial problems are one of the biggest causes of divorce.

It shocks me how many clients come in to initial consultations with no firm grasp on their family's finances. They're not sure if their spouses have pensions or other types of retirement accounts, they don't have a family budget, and they're unsure even whether their cars are leased or owned.

It's very difficult to divide assets if you don't know what assets you have. The discovery process will help unearth such issues in a divorce, but it's something all couples (whether contemplating divorce or happily married) should understand. This includes insurance (health, life, and so on) in case something bad happens that will affect family finances.

Such personal financial knowledge is particularly important in divorce cases, but I encourage everyone to have monthly discussions of budget and finance and write down all their assets of all types so they have a clear financial picture of their households. Having these ready for a divorce consultation is extremely helpful.

## WORK AS A TEAM

Not to get all Pollyanna again, but working together (whether happily married or not) can lead to better results for all involved. If you have an uphill battle with debt as my wife and I did with our student loans, you can either bury your head in the sand or team up and fight together. Every time we cut down our

I encourage **everyone** to have monthly discussions of budget and finance and write down all their assets of all types so they have a clear financial picture of their households.

student loans by $1,000, my wife and I would cross off a box on a chart we created. It took us eight years, but we eventually crossed off that last box. We didn't let ourselves get all stressed out; we just found ways together to be frugal, and that teamwork strengthened our marriage.

Even divorcing couples can give some thought to their situations. Maybe they can agree to remain in the marital house; maybe they can be reasonable in their divorce demands and avoid wasting thousands on legal fees to end up with furniture that's worth $500. Fighting spouses can hurt themselves more than they hurt their spouses.

After your divorce, you'll likely date again, and statistically, the odds are that you'll remarry. This type of mind-set change can help make your post-divorce life more satisfying. You want to learn from the issues that plagued your first relationship, and you don't want to make the same mistakes again. That is not the pathway to living Happily *Even* After.

## DON'T BE JUDGMENTAL

It's common for spouses to have different opinions about personal finances. My wife and I have different tolerances for risk. I like to invest most of our funds in stocks whereas she prefers a larger emergency fund than I do and putting money into bonds or other safer investments. So we work together to find common ground (not always achieved), and we attempt to be supportive even if investments or decisions are ultimately proven to be less advantageous than we'd hoped.

## LEARN

I can't expect everyone to be a personal finance dork as I am, but all our finances are increasingly important today. Perhaps you can take turns becoming knowledgeable about different financial matters and reporting to each other about what you've learned. For instance, one can focus on being frugal while the other figures out the best way to manage the resulting savings.

## KEEP GOOD NOTES AND SAVE DOCUMENTS

Finally, and particularly in tax season, keep good notes and properly maintain documents pertaining to all your finances.

Personal finance and money issues may not be the cause of divorce in all cases, but I've noticed a lack of communication and money stress as being telling symptoms of an upcoming divorce with many of my clients.

Whether you're happily married or pursuing divorce, it's important to keep some of the above ideas in mind to help you achieve the best outcome for you and your family.

If you're handling your own finances post-divorce for the first time in a while, make sure you read up on the subject and talk with accountants or other experts as necessary to make sure your finances are in good working order. I've fought hard with many clients to preserve their assets only to later learn post-divorce that they made regrettable decisions.

As soon as your divorce is finalized, get a new will drafted, follow up with your divorce terms to obtain your assets, and learn about personal finance if it's not in your wheelhouse to make sure you can properly preserve the divided assets, pay off your share of the marital debt, and have significant cash flow for yourself and your children.

## CONSIDER USING A PARENTING COORDINATOR POST-DIVORCE

Making day-to-day parenting decisions can be difficult enough in an intact family. I grew up in a family that allowed me to watch PG or even PG-13 movies at a young age while my wife remembers her mother fast-forwarding through the scary scenes in even Disney movies.

One parent might not want a child to watch a particular *Star Wars* movie while the other doesn't mind that. One parent might think it's okay for a child to have a soda at a party while the other might think milk is more appropriate. Such relatively minor little issues can raise debates in all families; divorced couples will still have to engage in such decisions, so part of living Happily *Even* After is being able to effectively coparent. At times, a parenting coordinator—think referee—could help. Even the threat of bringing one in could make the difference between post-divorce litigation and headaches or appropriate and sensible compromise. A good parenting coordinator can really be a game-changer for those who require additional incentive in spite of the cost. It can cut down on children trying to game the systems—plural—when they're spending time in two different households; they'll quickly figure out which parent is the pushover for this or that.

Both exes could agree on hiring a parenting coordinator, and the court might rule that one is necessary. As defined in the

Overview section of the Program Standards for the Parenting Coordinator Guidelines (Pilot Program, 2007),

> A Parenting Coordinator is a qualified neutral person appointed by the court, or agreed to by the parties, to facilitate the resolution of day to day parenting issues that frequently arise within the context of family life when parents are separated. The court may appoint a Parenting Coordinator at any time during a case involving minor children after a parenting plan has been established when the parties cannot resolve these issues on their own. The Parenting Coordinator's goal is to aid parties in monitoring the existing parenting plan, reducing misunderstandings, clarifying priorities, exploring possibilities for compromise and developing methods of communication that promote collaboration in parenting. The Parenting Coordinator's role is to facilitate decision making between the parties or make such recommendations, as may be appropriate, when the parties are unable to do so. One primary goal of the Parenting Coordinator is to empower parents to develop and utilize effective parenting skills so that they can resume the parenting and decision-making role without the need for outside intervention. The Parenting Coordinator should provide guidance and direction to the parties with the primary focus on the best interests of the child by reducing conflict and fostering sound decisions that aid positive child development.

This pilot program for parenting coordinators ended in 2012 in New Jersey, but courts may still appoint them and parties may still agree to utilize them. Parenting coordinators will generally have a mental health, social work, or divorce law background, and they can be a great option.

The primary role of such coordinators is to facilitate communication between the divorced parties regarding parenting issues. They don't take the place of a judge and cannot enforce or modify any orders, but they can work within the confines and parameters of any active agreements between the parties serving as a neutral party.

## A WORD ON PRENUPTIAL AGREEMENTS FOR THOSE WHO INTEND ON REMARRYING

I consider prenuptial agreements (also known as a premarital agreements or antenuptial agreements) to be the most tricky document to negotiate in the realm of family and divorce law. This is because too much negotiating can upset an otherwise happy couple. However, prenuptial agreements are becoming increasingly common even among middle-class couples. Just as in a divorce, each party will have their own attorney in a New Jersey prenuptial agreement. Many of my clients that get a divorce comment that they wish they had a prenup the first time around. Although remarriage may seem an awfully distant idea for most of you reading this book, keep prenuptial agreements in mind should you one day remarry.

In my Flemington, New Jersey family law practice, I get involved in negotiating prenuptial agreements for couples contemplating marriage but looking to set specific parameters in the event of their divorce or the passing of one of them. (Both parties are represented by different attorneys just as in a divorce.)

Although prenuptial agreements are more common in second marriages or where one or both parties have accumulated substantial wealth, prenups are becoming increasingly common among all age groups and asset classes. That said, there is often only one party who wants a prenup, and at times, it's one of their parents.

With all that said, what should you do if you're engaged and your spouse asks you to enter into a prenuptial agreement or you want one? First, we must define a prenup—a form of a contract setting forth an understanding between the parties about their marriage and the end of their marriage. It is required that this agreement be made *prior* to the marriage (although reconciliation and post-nuptial agreements are sometimes contemplated by New Jersey law). It becomes enforceable only after the parties actually marry. Such agreements can be quite simple or very complex. As a form of contract, the parties are given great leeway in drafting the agreement's specific terms and language.

To be valid in New Jersey, a prenup must be in writing or it won't be enforceable. They must also have a statement of assets attached to it. As is the case in most contracts, consideration—something of value—must be given, and the agreement must also be signed by both parties so it will be legally binding after they actually marry.

Under the Uniform Premarital Agreement Act, the parties may contract respecting some of the following issues

- rights and obligations relating to real property and the disposition of such property
- choice of venue and jurisdiction
- spousal support

Note that prenuptial agreements cannot waive a child's right to support from either parent and cannot address custody or parenting-time issues.

To be enforceable, a prenuptial agreement cannot be wildly unreasonable or signed under duress, and both parties must have had sufficient time to review and negotiate it with the help of independent counsel. If one party later seeks to revoke it, that party has the responsibility to demonstrate why it should be revoked.

Certain protections are in place in New Jersey even after a prenup is signed. For instance, noncommingled premarital property generally remains separate property in New Jersey. So if you own free and clear a home in your name and do not commingle that asset (or allow your new spouse to provide sweat equity into, say, its remodeling), it should generally remain separate regarding equitable distribution if you later divorce. The same goes with property you're given or inherit and certain amounts of personal-injury awards as I mentioned earlier.

## SHOULD I SIGN A PRENUP?

Those basics out of the way, what should you do if your spouse wants a prenup? First, it's important not to take the suggestion of a prenuptial agreement personally or as an indictment of your relationship or your fiancé or fiancée's trust in you. There are many reasons to seek a prenuptial agreement, and not all of them are negative. As noted above, it's a growing trend that helps provide some control to both parties to determine what would occur in a worst-case outcome. Risk-adverse people may consider it nothing more than a reasonable request.

Discuss any concerns you have with your intended to get a sense of his or her motivations. You may decide that a prenup just isn't necessary. But if concerns linger, make sure you both have an understanding of the process to be utilized and the reasons behind the request to not strain your relationship.

If your spouse-to-be insists on a prenup, make sure you get your own lawyer to review it and help you negotiate its terms if that's necessary. Don't allow your future spouse or his or her attorney to select your attorney for you. It might seem okay at the time, but that could lead you to feel cheated and upset by the process later on even if everyone was operating in good faith.

Make sure your attorney fully explains the process to you along with the specific repercussions of what you intend to sign. You should end up with a firm understanding of what the law would be if you do and if you don't sign a prenup so you can understand what you stand to gain or lose by signing it. A prenup might call for a permanent waiver of alimony, and based on incomes and the length of the marriage, that could be a huge amount to give up.

You should review the entire contract through that prism and then view it globally to determine if it's reasonable and fair. There is no requirement that the agreement be fair, just that it not be so unfair as to be unconscionable at the time the agreement was signed.

You should work with your attorney to provide financial documentation (and to review financial documentation from your spouse) as this is a requirement of a prenuptial agreement and will help you determine whether the proposed prenuptial agreement language is fair.

Never be afraid to voice your concerns to your lawyer and to negotiate the matter and even aggressively if required. Keep in mind that if your fiancé or fiancée is the one seeking a prenup, that's because he or she is looking to protect his or her interests by means of a prenup, so your protecting your interests shouldn't be an issue, and no one's feelings should end up hurt. So get some assistance and make sure you're protecting your interests. You might regret it later on if you let the bliss of upcoming nuptials silence your valid concerns.

And important—just as you would want to with any other legal document, don't sign it or waive any rights until a lawyer who's on your side only has looked it over and has pointed out all its legal ramifications and their pros and cons.

I've heard too many clients say they wish they had gotten a prenup before they'd married. I believe prenups can be an important safeguard. Many of those who have been divorced will readily agree to that.

## CHAPTER 27

# *When Your Ex's Baggage Threatens Your Happily **Even** After*

When children are involved, there are few things more frightening than learning your ex is using drugs again, relapsing into alcohol abuse, or having a mental breakdown or psychotic episode. This chapter covers some of the legal steps you can take if you find yourself in such a situation so you can best preserve your children's safety and happiness as well as yours.

## THE IMPACT OF DRUGS AND MENTAL HEALTH ISSUES ON A MARRIAGE

As a divorce lawyer practicing in central New Jersey, I find that my clients tend to reflect the demographics of the region; many of them have good jobs and significant resources. Nevertheless, mental health and drug and alcohol abuse issues tend to be present across all demographics. Addiction and mental health issues are common, and they can be the (sometimes unspoken) impetus for a divorce.

When children are concerned, there may have to be significant negotiations regarding custody and parenting-time issues; under New Jersey law, you could be found guilty of neglect or child endangerment for leaving children with an intoxicated spouse.

The Divorce Agreement in such circumstances will often require certain steps on the part of the spouse who is using drugs, drinking too much, or has mental health issues to be supervised during visits with his or her children—perhaps mandatory AA classes, drug tests, and other requirements.

If substance abuse or mental health issues arise after a divorce, you will have some options. If your ex shows up intoxicated or high, you can consider recording or videotaping the behavior, make notes of all the details immediately, and even contact the police or DCPP as appropriate.

You can also file motions or Orders to Show Cause if it's an urgent matter to get the courts involved quickly. Keep in mind, however, that courts generally frown on what they might consider self-help actions such as withholding your children, but the courts could at least temporarily suspend parenting time or require supervised parenting time.

## PURSUE LEGAL ACTIONS WHILE EVIDENCE IS STRONGEST

A lot of drug and alcohol abuse and mental health issues are cyclical in nature. By the time you decide to take action, your ex might appear to be on the straight and narrow again, and you'll be left wondering what you'll do when the problem arises again. Taking action when your spouse is committed, is in rehab, or is otherwise at his or her worst can help courts or agencies understand the severity of the situation and lean toward taking appropriate actions so that "next time" doesn't occur for your and your children's safety.

Courts and lawyers will never be able to move as quickly as the police can if a crime is being committed or if you and your children are in danger, so never hesitate to make that 911 call.

As long as your children are children, you'll never be completely free of your ex, but never let his or her negative actions harm them or you—nip issues in the bud.

# CHAPTER 28

# Post-Divorce Out-of-State Relocation and Removal Law

**One thing** most of us take for granted is the ability to live anywhere we choose. Moving can mean uprooting your family, changing your job, or otherwise going on an adventure. But for those who are divorced or separated, moving out of state with children can also trigger serious legal considerations.

## REMOVAL LAW IN NEW JERSEY

In New Jersey, removal law provides that when the superior court has jurisdiction over the custody and maintenance of minor children of parents divorced, separated, or living apart, they "shall not be removed out of its jurisdiction against their own consent, if of suitable age to signify same, nor while under that age without the consent of both parents, unless the court shall otherwise order."[20]

The court addressed some of the differences between parents who share physical custody whether it was court ordered or agreed upon by the exes and a parent who has primary

---

20  N.J.S.A., 9:2-2.

physical custody and the other has secondary or alternate physical custody.

> In a child custody modification context in determining the standard to be applied to a parent's removal application, **the focus of the inquiry is whether the physical custodial relationship among parents is one in which one parent is the "primary caretaker" and the other is the "secondary caretaker." If so, the removal application must be analyzed in accordance with the criteria outlined in** *Baures*. **(emphasis added)**[21]

In a child-custody modification context, if the parents truly share both legal and physical custody, an application by one parent to relocate with the child out of state will be considered a change of custody. The relocating parent will have to demonstrate that such a move is in the best interests of the child. If one parent is the primary physical custodian, however, if that parent can demonstrate he or she is not leaving the state for bad-faith reasons, the noncustodial parent has to prove that the move wouldn't be in the child's best interests. Thus the first step of a removal test considers the type of parenting arrangement between the parties.

A removal motion by a party in a case in which children rotate between houses with each parent assuming full parental responsibility half the time is clearly an application to change a custodial status that cannot be maintained from a distance. In contrast, an application by a custodial parent to move away in a case in which the noncustodial parent sees the children once or twice a week and is not seeking to change that state of affairs is a removal motion. The possible scenarios are limitless and are

---

21    *O'Connor v. O'Connor*, 349 N.J. Super, 381.

all based on many facts, but what's in the best interests of the children will generally trump anything else.

Let's imagine a case in which the plaintiff, the parent of primary residence, is seeking to relocate to New York not far from New Jersey so the other parent's parenting time will not be interfered with much if at all. But if the matter of relocation becomes contentious, according to the law, the court will review how these factors come into play.

1. the reasons given for the move
2. the reasons given for the opposition
3. the past history of dealings between the parties insofar as it bears on the reasons advanced by both parties for supporting and opposing the move
4. whether the child will receive educational, health, and leisure opportunities at least equal to what is available at their current location
5. any special needs or talents of the child that require accommodation
6. whether a visitation and communication schedule can be developed that will allow the noncustodial parent to maintain a full and continue relationship
7. the likelihood that the custodial parent will continue to foster the child's relationship with the noncustodial parent
8. the effect of the move on extended family relationships
9. if the child is of age, his or her preference
10. whether the child is entering his or her senior year in high school

11. whether the noncustodial parent has the ability to relocate

12. any other factor bearing on the child's interest

Leaving for legitimate reasons such as a change in work or to be close to family will be viewed in a better light than merely a desire to leave the state.

The noncustodial parent may leave the state any time, but doing so would likely subject him or her to a motion to change parenting time.

The law in this area is constantly changing and very fact-sensitive, so it's best to discuss these issues with an attorney before you start planning to relocate.

## AFTER THE DIVORCE: STORE YOUR IMPORTANT DOCUMENTS IN A SAFE PLACE

For obvious reasons, there is a sense of closure associated with the finalization of a divorce. There are, however, many ways the case may be revisited particularly via post-judgment motions as I've already gone over. For some, the divorce decree will be the final court action, but for others, divorce issues—as we have seen—can continue off and on for many years. These can include requests to modify child support or alimony, the emancipation of a child, retirement issues, college costs, health-care reimbursement issues, and others.

The biggest mistakes I see people make when filing *pro se* (by themselves) motions is they fail to provide adequate documentation. In most instances, an original and a new Case Information Statement, a copy of the Marital Settlement Agreement, and recent orders are required. Without these documents, a court will often deny requests for relief.

Letting the aftereffects of a divorce linger for years is not my definition of living Happily *Even* After. All too often, people are in a rush to get their divorce finalized, don't address all terms, or don't retain attorneys, and then they have Divorce Agreements that make little or no sense and cause ongoing issues.

Here's a list—though it's not exhaustive—of what documents you should carefully save and be able to put your hands on quickly.

- an original (from the time of the divorce, etc.) of the Case Information Statement. For most types of modification and other motions, a new Case Information Statement will also need to be appended to a Motion
- an original (gold-sealed) Divorce Agreement (aka Marital Settlement Agreement, Property Settlement Agreement) and divorce decree
- original child-support guidelines
- any other orders including Consent Orders entered by the court or between the parties
- receipts or other proof of child-support or medical expenses, college expenses, etc. paid or received
- bank account or other documentation as to joint accounts or when held in the name of or for the benefit of a child
- federal income tax returns, W-2s, and pay stubs
- proof of job searches (if attempting to later prove loss of employment or change of circumstances involving employment)

You'll need a lot of the above if you want to talk with an attorney about possible post-judgment motions or actions. Keep the originals in a binder that you put in safe and private place, and put copies in perhaps a safety deposit box or scan them and put them in the "cloud."

In short, even after a divorce is finalized, prepare as though it's not the end of the legal issues between you and your ex though I hope you're doing so is merely that.

# Conclusion

I hope this book has given you a better understanding not only of the nuts and bolts of New Jersey divorce law and procedure but also how the human element of a divorce can make or break your chances of success.

We humans relish control, but in a divorce, some things are simply beyond our control. We don't know how the other side or the court will respond to this motion or that request. We can, however, control our thoughts, emotions, and actions, move forward in the right spirit, and seek the most advantageous yet reasonable approaches available.

It's only human to feel negative emotions such as anger, frustration, disappointment, jealousy, and guilt during a New Jersey divorce. Even I am not immune to such feelings when I'm handling a divorce case. But it's ultimately more effective—and a lot cheaper—to take those emotions out in a healthy way. So trash a guitar, take a long run, or hit a punching bag. You and your children will be better off in the long run.

If there's one main point I hoped to get across in this book, it's that emotion is the largest X-factor in a divorce. How you bob and weave through the difficult process will have a great impact on your post-divorce life and happiness. Your attorney will be important, but nobody will have a greater impact on your divorce or play a more important role in it than you will.

Like Virgil, I stand ready to help you and be your guide through treacherous pathways and seemingly hopeless times. And I want nothing more than to see you get through to your own personal version of paradise and live Happily *Even* After.

**Thanks for reading my book.** If you're considering a New Jersey divorce or family law action, contact me to discuss your options. You can schedule an initial consultation by calling my office at 908-237-3096 or by scheduling your own consult on my firm's website, www.mynjdivorcelawyer.com.

# Why Choose Carl Taylor Law, LLC?

**Finding the right attorney** is an important decision—one that you should take very seriously. Considering the number of talented lawyers in New Jersey, you might find it difficult to find the right one for your case. But there's nothing I enjoy more than working with clients. I find it an honor and a privilege to be an attorney. I work tirelessly for the satisfaction of my clients, and I enjoy righting wrongs, making my clients whole again, and leaving them in a better position than when they first walked through my door.

I consider my ability to exert a positive influence on my community as well as my clients a real privilege and a responsibility that I take very seriously.

I stand ready to answer your questions, work toward the results you desire, and give my all to be a shining light during a dark time in my clients' lives. Like Virgil in Dante's *Inferno*, I stand ready to work with you through the toughest of times to guide you to the light of a brighter future.

I hope that whether you contact our firm or not that you enjoyed this book and will seek to incorporate some of its ideals into your New Jersey divorce or serious family law matter. I wish you all the best in finding your Happily *Even* After.

Very truly yours,
*Carl A. Taylor III, Esq.*

# Please contact our firm to learn more at

## 908-237-3096

## www.mynjdivorcelawyer.com

# CARL TAYLOR LAW

908-237-3096
WWW.MYNJDIVORCELAWYER.COM

Country Side Plaza North
361 State Route 31
Building E, Suite 1501
Flemington, NJ 08822